RISE & FALL
OF A
POLITICAL
ANIMAL

a memoir

RISE & FALL
OF A
POLITICAL
ANIMAL

a memoir

BY SIDNEY GREEN

GREAT PLAINS
PUBLICATIONS

Great Plains Publications
420 – 70 Arthur Street
Winnipeg, MB R3B 1G7
www.greatplains.mb.ca

Great Plains Publications gratefully acknowledges the financial support
provided for its publishing program by the Government of Canada through
the Book Publishing Industry Development Program (BPIDP); the Canada
Council for the Arts; as well as the Manitoba Department of Culture,
Heritage and Tourism; and the Manitoba Arts Council.

Design & Typography by Gallant Design Ltd.

Printed in Canada by Kromar Printing

CANADIAN CATALOGUING IN PUBLICATION DATA

Main entry under title:

Green, Sid
  Rise and fall of a political animal : a memoir / Sid Green.

Includes index.
ISBN 1-894283-43-0

  I. Green, Sid.   2. Politicians—Manitoba—Biography.   3. New
Democratic Party of Manitoba—Biography.
I. Title.
FC3378.1.G73A3   2003   971.27'03'092   C2003-910905-4

To Nathan, Ruth, Roslyn, David, Diana, Michael, Aaron, Joshua, Emma, Shivaun, Charlie, Matthew, Bennie, Kelly, and Jane.

CONTENTS

FOREWORD

As a young politician, Sid Green would accept any invitation, any at all. A group of six was enough to attract the spirited, passionate Green, who believed that inspiring a single person justified a trek, near or distant. That never changed, and the reader of this memoir will catch the passion on every page.

He did it for one simple reason; he wanted power. He says so in this book and he makes no apologies for it. He wanted power because that's what he needed to make things better. He wanted power to keep others from having power over him. As Green himself says, "In my view, the only way to avoid being controlled was to control the power."

The story of The New Democratic Party's rise to power, vaulting from third place to first in 1969, has not been well told yet. Sid Green's personal account adds an important voice that will interest historians as this period becomes the subject of academic review. It was a dynamic period and one in which Sid Green was a major player. He tells the story from an intensely personal perspective. Hardly a page goes by without commentary on the individuals who were with him or against him. Few punches are pulled here. This is a full account of the dynamics of the political process – the disappointments, the victories, the setbacks, the frustrations, the betrayals.

Although Sid Green began as a committed New Democrat and ended his career as a frustrated Progressive, he would be the first to say that his ideas did not change. His stormy relationship with the union movement after he left the New Democratic Party is the best example of how Green's approach to issues could turn friends into enemies in the blink of an eye. They changed – he didn't.

He takes us inside the cabinet room, a mysterious place for most, to understand the way in which consensus is achieved, how dominant personalities can carry an argument, and what sorts of pressure works on premiers, in this case Ed Schreyer, who led the New Democrats in power from 1969 to 1977. This was a period in Manitoba history when huge battles were fought. Automobile insurance was taken over by a provincial agency, medicare premums were scrapped in favour of tax hikes, northern Hydro development became an integral part of the economic agenda of the province, and public monies were used to stimulate industrial development.

Green remembers the full public galleries and the public debate that swirled around the controversial issues chosen by the government he served. He remembers with impressive clarity who was on what side of these issues, inside the government and outside. He offers insightful commentary about what was motivating all the players and who won the day and why.

Green's political experience began as a municipal councillor and ended as a member of the legislature, but throughout his career, he was fascinated by national issues, especially those that dealt with the very essence of Canadian federalism, namely the importance of two official languages, the relative power between Parliament and the courts and the fundamental rights of individuals. His descriptions of relationships among governments offers a refreshing insight into jurisdictional battles that have been so much a part of Canada's public discussion.

The constant tension in this book is the one between ideas and personalities – how firm alliances fade, how friendships can be strained and how politicians on opposite sides of the house can from time to time join in common cause when ideology trumps partisanship. A good example of this can be found in Green's respect for former Progressive Conservative Premier Sterling Lyon, particularly on the issue of the supremacy of Parliament.

Green read the newspapers faithfully. He sites them frequently in this book to reflect the public mood at the time he was a central figure. This is a good reminder to journalists that what they write counts and is often clipped. Green clipped and what was said counted to him. Green's account of some relationships he developed with journalists and his attitude toward the media in general add a dimension that will shed some light on the intriguing dynamic between those who govern and those who report and comment.

This is a book that had to be written. Green had to do many things in his colourful career in public life. He was compelled every step of the way by a belief in what he thought was the right thing to do and by a fierce energy to see that it was done. Sometimes it was, sometimes it wasn't, but through success and failure, the reader will conclude that this was a formidable career in Manitoba politics. Now through this volume the reader can assess the breadth and depth of Sid Green's contribution to public life.

—Jim Carr

PREFACE

Events covered by this work occurred between 1961 and 1991. For the most part they relate to politics in the Province of Manitoba and to a lesser extent, the national scene.

After pondering as to whether or not I would undertake this project, I finally decided to do so for two essential reasons. Most importantly, there are people close to me, particularly fifteen grandchildren, who are only vaguely aware of the fact that their grandfather was involved in politics in Manitoba. Because I have never really discussed that participation with them, my substantial successes and ultimate defeat are a relative mystery to them. I am egocentric enough to want them to have access to my version of the facts.

Secondly, and of almost equal importance, is the need to tell the inside story of the New Democratic Party's rise to power in the Province of Manitoba and its period in government. There are, of course, news stories about what occurred from 1969 to 1977 and conventional wisdom about the reasons behind what happened. However most of the knowledge gleaned from the media fails to present an accurate picture.

It is strange that so little of a serious nature has been written on the subject. The history of the New Democratic Party's rise to power in Manitoba and its time in government is of some political importance and significance. Its election in 1969 was only the second time the NDP achieved power in Canada. The first was in Saskatchewan, where the party had and still has a record of power.

While New Democrats had broad support in Saskatchewan, the situation was different in Manitoba where the party had a sound but concentrated base. As a result, a relatively small number of candidates usually were elected and re-elected. This was far better than what was occurring to the NDP in Alberta and the Maritimes, but the numbers paled in comparison to those in British

Columbia or even Ontario. Nevertheless the Manitoba party had steady and substantial support.

Given that situation, the prevailing attitude within the NDP in Manitoba was to revel in the role as the "conscience of the legislature." Party stalwarts never really believed they would achieve power. Nor did they have any genuine thirst to do so. The tone changed in the early 1960s and this discourse is intended to deal with the how and why the change came about.

I am well aware that there is danger of egotistical subjectivity in writing about one's own participation in events. I measured this fact with what I considered to be the need for a more factual, historical accounting of what occurred, as distinct from the mythology which I know for the most part to be inaccurate.

It is also of some importance to describe the vagaries of political life, notably my own success in the political world and ultimate defeat. The measure of success in politics is obtaining and retaining power. I was involved in obtaining power but was then removed by the electorate. An understanding of how success and failure can be the result of political ideals, which remained essentially the same throughout my life, is an interesting study. I am sufficiently immodest to believe that it can form a contribution to the political history of Manitoba.

Autobiographies or memoirs are a real challenge to those who write them. Objectivity about oneself is, of course, not attainable. I do not claim this to be an objective story. It is my story. Some people may resent this work and argue about its credibility. I decided that it is more important to tell the story and risk criticism and challenges than not to tell it at all. Over the years and particularly with respect to my leadership contests, much has been said by my opponents which is false. This work is intended to put my side of the story on record.

Numerous people who participated in the events described in this account can verify its accuracy and I am sure they will do so. They include Sam Uskiw, Ben Hanuschak, Herb Schultz, and Murdoch MacKay.

Several people deserve recognition and appreciation for the assistance which they have given me in completing this work. My secretary, Mary Ann Russell was required to listen, decipher, and attempt to properly arrange numerous dictation tapes. She then had to type and retype several edited and re-edited copies. Victor Olson, a university lecturer, did an extensive and splendid job of research to ensure accuracy. Arlene Billinkoff, a former legislative reporter did the painstaking and painful work of editing my grammar.

I would also like to express my appreciation to the Winnipeg Steeler Hockey Team which gave me the youth and energy to complete this work.

—Sidney Green

PART ONE

POLITICAL DEBUT

THE BEGINNING

I n 1960 I was a young Winnipeg lawyer with an office in the Confederation Building on Main Street across from the City Hall.

One day a message on my desk indicated a call from Stephen Lewis. That name was familiar to most politically active people within the ranks of the CCF (Canadian Commonwealth Federation) in Ontario and nationally. He was the dynamic oldest sibling in the family of David Lewis, an Ontario lawyer who was an institution in the CCF. Not only had Stephen's father been the secretary of the national party, he was generally considered to be its most powerful and influential person.

Having heard a great deal about the younger Lewis and eager to meet him, I quickly returned the call and made an appointment. Shortly thereafter we met in my office, where Lewis urged me to become involved in the new political party then being formed. He also sought a financial contribution.

Despite a keen and probably ambitious interest in political affairs, I had never been associated with any political party. I had never found a political "home."

Raised in the north end of Winnipeg, I lived on Selkirk Avenue for my first 22 years. The area was a hot-bed of politics with proponents of socialism opposed by ethnic nationalists. Residents elected municipal, provincial and federal representatives who were generally Socialist, CCF, Communist or Nationalist.

This was understandable in the working class area between 1929 and 1951. It was populated primarily by depression-oriented people who sympathized with the socialist message that 'some people worked too little and got too much and others worked too hard and got too little'.

The inequities of society were generally attributed to the unfairness of the capitalist system. There was a genuine belief that society could be reorganized for the benefit of mankind generally and the disadvantaged in particular. This atmosphere in which I grew up was reflected in most of my political opinions. I was generally regarded as somewhat of a radical, a maverick and "shit disturber", having spoken out in support of left-wing positions. However I had never joined any political party.

I worked as an articling law student with Joseph Zuken, a Communist school trustee and subsequently an alderman. My positions in law school were generally anti-establishment but any interaction with Communists turned me off, largely because of their seemingly self-righteous attitudes and apparent espousal of the Soviet party line.

On the other hand I regarded the CCF as a somewhat wishy-washy organization. This was particularly apparent when the party purged from its ranks three Manitoba MLAs whom it accused of having Communist leanings. In 1945 D.L. Johnson was expelled by the provincial convention. In 1949 David Lewis was one of the chief engineers in the expulsion of Barry Richards and William Doneleyko. The moves proved to be ineffective and probably lost, rather than gained, party supporters.

On the national scene, the CCF had been decimated by John Diefenbaker's second electoral victory in 1958. The party's representation in the House of Commons was reduced to eight and the leader M.J. Coldwell, was defeated in his own riding.

Also defeated were Stanley Knowles in Winnipeg North and Allistair Stewart in Winnipeg North Centre. The loss of these two seats and such high-profile distinguished representatives was a calamity. Knowles lost to John McLean while Stewart lost to Murray Smith. The latter victory demonstrated the extent of the Diefenbaker appeal. Smith was completely unknown in North Winnipeg and had been named as a candidate simply to fill the slate.

The loss of Knowles was a disaster, a pill too bitter to be swallowed by the power brokers, such as they were, in the CCF. Shortly thereafter he was hired by the Canadian Labour Congress as a special consultant. His responsibilities included the formation of a political alliance consisting of all forces on the democratic left – essentially the trade union movement and the CCF.

Knowles and other CCFers embarked on this project in order to prepare what was quickly becoming known as the "new party" for the federal election expected in 1962. Stephen Lewis was one of its activists.

When Lewis walked into my office it was the first but definitely not the last time that we would meet and discuss politics. With considerable enthusiasm, Lewis quickly explained that people like me should be involved with the new party both actively and as a financial supporter. When discussing financial support he did not speak in modest terms. He wanted a substantial contribution and made it clear that it was the objective of the new party to form a government in Canada.

I had never before met anybody with such enthusiasm and optimism for his project. Lewis appeared to believe sincerely in everything he was saying and expected that his own mood would be contagious. It was.

Although nothing definitive was done immediately it was probably at that moment that I decided to abandon political dalliance and get involved in a meaningful way. This attitude was reinforced by a junket with my partner Leon Mitchell to a trade union conference in Calgary. At that time I was a practising lawyer with three children and was looking forward to a promising law career.

Mitchell, who was called to the bar in September of 1955, the same day as I, had an interesting history. Raised in Winkler, Manitoba, he later moved to Winnipeg where his father opened a grocery store at McKenzie Street and Selkirk Avenue, just one block from the Green residence. But we did not meet until our joint call to the bar.

Before that meeting Mitchell was involved in the trade union movement and was a highly respected business agent for the Federation of Civic Employees. As the main strategist for the threatened strike in Winnipeg in 1952, he was largely credited with achievements made in that labour dispute.

In 1950 Mitchell nearly died during the Winnipeg polio epidemic. He managed to survive largely by strength of will. By the time he was called to the bar he could walk with the assistance of two aluminum canes. Although physically weakened he maintained a strength of character and will power which gave him an advantage over many who were physically fit.

He opened an office in the Confederation Building at almost the same time I started a practice in the same building. Mitchell had many clients but not much actual legal experience. On the other hand, I had intense articling experience but very few clients.

We met for coffee on several occasions and a relationship seemed to fall neatly into place. By the spring of 1956 we shared offices and within a few years were partners. The practice flourished and in a short period of time became known as the most prominent labour relations firm in Manitoba. I did most of the litigation while Mitchell focused on negotiations, arbitrations and related matters.

When we went to the Calgary conference I not only rubbed shoulders with labour people and political notables in the CCF, but also heard a speech by T.C. (Tommy) Douglas, then premier of Saskatchewan.

To say that Douglas' speech was electrifying is an understatement. I saw not only an unparalleled captivator of audiences, but also a practical politician who had ideals which he knew how to implement. This was apparent in his record. He was premier of a province which had already introduced the first universal hospital plan in Canada and was on its way to providing a comprehensive universal, publicly financed medical care program. The Douglas government also facilitated the first compulsory and universal public automobile insurance underwriting. These were the kinds of things that I believed were needed in order to provide equity to all people.

FIRST PLUNGE

Shortly after the visit with Stephen Lewis, I received a message saying that Lloyd Stinson had called. The name was well known. Stinson had been the distinguished leader of the CCF in Manitoba and sat in the provincial legislature from 1945 until he was defeated in the Roblin victory of June 16, 1958.

Stinson, a former church minister, was highly respected and was a formidable political figure. He had presence, intelligence and exceptional speaking ability. His one political weakness was an apparent lack of will to supplant the government.

Instead, he and many CCFers at the time preferred to rationalize their third-place standing by making a virtue of it. They comforted themselves with the myth that they were not successful because they were morally superior and above the kind of politics necessary to achieve power. They revelled in the notion that they were the conscience of the legislature.

Despite his defeat, Stinson maintained an active interest in politics. He had been the CCF standard bearer in the federal riding of Winnipeg-South, a large and, in some areas, very affluent riding. The CCF traditionally ran a distant third to the free-enterprise Liberal and Conservative parties.

Excited about the call from Stinson, I quickly responded and an appointment was set up. When Stinson arrived, he quickly came to the point. As suspected, he wanted to discuss the possibility of me becoming a candidate for the New Democratic Party. Like any other human being, I was flattered and pleased by the attention.

A federal election was expected shortly. The new NDP had recently been officially formed in Ottawa and Tommy Douglas had agreed to become its leader. It was typical of his conviction and dedication that Douglas resigned the premiership of Saskatchewan, a position he would probably have retained indefinitely. He became the leader of a party which technically had no seats in the House of Commons although its predecessor had held eight seats after the Diefenbaker victory in 1958.

The CCF had received only about 9.5 per cent of the popular vote but there was optimism about the new party, which, through the efforts of Stanley Knowles, had been fashioned by the labour movement and the old party.

Given Douglas' leadership and the enthusiasm which was being generated across the country, it seemed likely the NDP would make a significant debut into Canadian politics at the general election expected in 1962.

Stinson's proposal that I run as the party candidate in Winnipeg South was flattering, but it was no political prize. It was more like leading a lamb to the slaughter. Since the CCF had never placed better than third in the riding, I may have been titillated by the idea but I expressed reservations.

A north-ender all my life, I had no identification with voters in the south end of the city. Furthermore my radical left-wing image might cause some embarrassment in a constituency about which I knew nothing.

Stinson dismissed the objections. As I later learned, active party members at the constituency level were far more radical than the spokesmen at the elected level. With some hesitation I accepted the invitation and placed myself at the disposal of the membership of the Winnipeg South constituency.

By objective standards and in retrospect, having me as a candidate in Winnipeg South was a political plus for the NDP. My credentials were solid. I was a reasonably prominent lawyer who had graduated from the Manitoba Law School with two gold medals and other prizes. I was a member of the boards of directors of the Red River Co-operative and the YMHA Community Centre. I had been the president of the Winnipeg Film Society and director of the B'nai Brith camp. In addition I had been active and was reasonably well known in public affairs. A candidate of my qualifications in a constituency where the NDP did not have a chance, spoke well of the new party's ability to attract people to public life.

The nominating meeting was duly held on May 9, 1962 at Osborne Hall, a modest CCF landmark which was one of the party's only tangible assets. By modern standards there was a fairly good attendance with approximately 50 people. The meeting was reported by both the *Winnipeg Free Press* and the *Winnipeg Tribune*.

In accepting the nomination, I gave a rather pedestrian speech on the philosophy of the NDP. I explained why I was attracted to it and what I would do if elected. In retrospect there was nothing newsworthy in the address, which was delivered more in the style of a lawyer then a politician trying to stimulate an audience.

During the question-and-answer period I was asked whether I saw any validity in those groups which were trying to pursue peace in what was then a troubled world. I responded by saying that since some people were successful in promoting a hate campaign it was just as logical to be successful in promoting a love campaign.

The *Free Press* reporter, who must have been bored to that point, eagerly seized on this casual remark as the basis of his story. The next day, eager to see whether my words of wisdom about NDP philosophy had been reported, I was devastated. The *Free Press* headline stated "Campaign of love is City NDP aim." The story said little about the current issues I had discussed.

Like any other candidate I was extremely sensitive to what the press was saying and believed the story was making a fool of me. I quickly called a friend, David Hunt, who worked for the *Free Press* and had agreed to help me with literature, press releases and public relations. After hearing my dismay about the way I had been treated, Hunt assured me the story would do no harm and it might do some good by making the public aware that I was running.

I also learned that, as an NDP candidate in a constituency such as Winnipeg South, I was not destined to receive much more public attention. The campaign was conducted vigorously and at the end of the day I received 7,793 votes, a credible showing since it was better than had ever been achieved by the CCF in that riding.

As for media recognition, there were only two newspaper stories of any consequence. The 'love' story was one. The second story involved a palmist. When it became known that the candidate had huge hands, a reporter, possibly nudged by Hunt, decided to do a human interest story. He arranged for me to go to the palmist and have my hand read. It resulted in a story in the *Winnipeg Free Press*, including a picture of me with outstretched hand and some of the palmist's inconsequential predictions.

Although I was not elected, there was no doubt that I had become a rising star in the NDP. The federal party won 19 seats and 13.4 per cent of the popular vote. However this progress was darkened by the fact that Tommy Douglas was defeated in his own riding. This problem was quickly rectified when British Columbia MP Ernie Regier resigned in order to create a by-election. Douglas won and took his place in the House of Commons as the leader of the NDP.

ELECTORAL SUCCESS

The 1962 federal election was a severe setback for the federal Conservatives. The Diefenbaker government, which lost its massive majority in the House of Commons, was clearly in trouble, mostly because of internal strife.

Eastern Tories had never fully accepted John Diefenbaker, whose decisions included the sale of grain to Red China and a refusal to accept U.S. nuclear weapons on Canadian soil. For the "boys from Bay Street" he was an embarrassment but the heaviest criticism came from party ranks.

In 1958 the Manitoba Conservatives had been elected to form a minority government in the wake of the Diefenbaker steamroller. Although they won a clear majority in 1959, there were indications that Premier Duff Roblin was nervous about the impact of the latest federal election since support for Diefenbaker had plummeted. Therefore he called a snap provincial election for December 14, 1962.

The date of that election caused me some embarrassment many years later. In March 1988 Howard Pawley called an election after his government was defeated when backbencher Jim Walding broke party ranks and voted against the NDP budget. I called the election a "Pawley snow job" because the campaign would take place during a Winnipeg winter.

Appearing on the Peter Warren show I was asked whether March was an appropriate time for an election. I responded by saying that any time was a good time for an election as long as you were out and somebody else was in. As an example I said, "Duff Roblin had an erection on December 14th." The answer was too delicious for Warren to censor, much to my dismay.

With a provincial election on the way in 1962, the NDP organization in the south Winnipeg riding of Osborne wanted me to be the candidate. I was an obvious choice since I had done a credible job in the federal riding which encompassed Osborne.

However, the request posed the same problems as the federal race. I was a north-ender and the NDP strength was based in that part of the city. To run in south Winnipeg was a sacrificial move which I had no chance of winning. While it would be regarded as a contribution to the party, it could also be dangerous to my political ambition, further removing me from my north-end image.

My partner, Leon Mitchell, and Lloyd Stinson agreed that it would be better for me to work within the party in the north end, with the expectation of receiving a nomination in that part of the city at some future date.

Meanwhile Saul Cherniack was nominated as the candidate in my home constituency of St. John's. The way had been cleared by David Orlikow's victory in the federal election, thus leaving his former provincial seat vacant.

I became the president of the constituency association and organized for the nomination. Cherniack was named by acclamation and resigned from Metro Council where he had represented Division Three (north Winnipeg), a seat which he had inherited from John Blumberg who had resigned to become the chairman of the Winnipeg Transit Commission.

It was like a game of musical chairs and once more there was a vacancy on Metro council. Although Metro constituencies were shaped like triangular slices of a pie with the point starting at the core of the city and then angling out to the farm areas on the outskirts, the majority of voters in this division lived in Winnipeg North.

I had never indicated any interest in municipal politics. In fact, I had been totally opposed to running. I had no desire in becoming preoccupied with administration, with little opportunity to make significant changes in social and economic policies. However the prospect of waiting four years for another provincial election without any exposure on a political platform did not appeal to me. After some persuasion by NDP president George Bain and the party's provincial secretary, Sam Goodman, I agreed to run for the Metro seat.

In the provincial election the Roblin government was returned to power while the NDP barely held its own with Russ Paulley as leader. Cherniack was easily elected in St. John's.

Because the Metro election followed closely on the provincial election, serious campaigning was almost impossible. Besides, it seemed that nobody gave a damn about the contest. Metro council itself was under constant attack by municipal councillors who made it a convenient scapegoat for every problem that they were not prepared to handle.

My nomination was a formality. No actual nominating meeting was held and the Inkster constituency riding was given the responsibility of conducting the campaign, such as it was.

I was well-known in the riding and had prominent exposure in various fields of endeavor. Not only was I endorsed by almost every local politician, including Knowles and Orlikow, I was also endorsed by the Manitoba Federation of Labour and the Winnipeg and District Labour Council in recognition of my legal battles on behalf of trade unions.

The only issue during the campaign which gained any prominence was a news release by Archie Micay, a spokesman for the Metro Election Committee. That group, probably dating back to the Winnipeg General Strike, was a loose coalition of private enterprisers who endorsed candidates at the municipal level. It had promoted candidates for city council and school board and expanded its activities to Metro when that body was created in the early 1960's. The committee's main purpose was to fight the left.

The Metro Election Committee nominated and endorsed John J. Thomas, a private investigator. Meanwhile the Communist party nominated Bill Kardash, a former MLA who had served the party with distinction and was a formidable debater. He had lost a leg in Spain while fighting against Franco in the 1930s.

Micay's news release warned that voter apathy could see a Communist elected to Metro Council. It wasn't quite clear as to whether he was identifying Kardash or me but the issue received considerable media attention.

I responded with my own news release, accusing Micay of using scare tactics in an attempt to divert public attention from the fact that the NDP had traditionally won the seat and was likely to hold it at the coming election. I was right. Voting resulted in 1,446 votes for me, 967 for Kardash and 919 for Thomas. When votes were transferred, I was elected.

The significant feature of the election was that, out of 28,450 eligible voters, only 3,078 (just over 10 per cent) cast ballots. While final figures gave me slightly more than 50 per cent of the vote I was actually elected by approximately 6 per cent of the eligible voters. This was hardly an overwhelming endorsement but it was a victory.

An interesting feature of the election was the number of people who were so upset with Metro government that they simply spoiled their ballots. I often remarked that, in this campaign, I barely defeated somebody named "Spoiled Ballot."

Although I had been less than enthusiastic about Metro Council, it was a fairly responsible position which should not be underrated. Ten councillors were elected to represent about 550,000 people. They had a significant budget and were responsible for many major administrative and infrastructure problems.

I was now a Metro councillor as well as a full-time lawyer. I was to fulfill these responsibilities for three years, while still playing a major role in activities of the NDP provincial organization.

METRO COUNCILLOR, 1962-1965

Between December 27, 1962 and August of 1965 I represented Division 3 of the Metropolitan Corporation of Greater Winnipeg Council. My tenure was fairly successful as I appeared to gain the respect of Chairman Dick Bonnycastle and fellow councillors. One was Art Coulter, a New Democrat and a trade unionist with whom I had worked on several labour cases. Coulter was subsequently instrumental in my appointment as a lecturer in labour law for business agents who were sent by their unions to the University of Manitoba for a special course.

As indicated, Metro council was not my cup of tea since its duties were primarily administrative. But at the same time I plunged headlong into provincial and federal NDP affairs.

As part of the provincial executive, I was heavily involved in the 1963 federal election. It was Diefenbaker's last stand and his minority government faced the challenge of the Liberals led by Lester B. Pearson. Many New Democrats feared a Liberal sweep similar to the Diefenbaker win of 1958, which would result in a drastic reduction of NDP representation.

I advanced the proposition, which I maintained throughout my political career, that by and large the public votes for or against the government. If voters want to oust the group in power they tend to choose the party most likely to win.

In 1963 this rationale meant the NDP would lose ground but I argued that the party should nominate a prominent list of candidates, even in ridings where there was not a hope of success. In particular, party luminaries Alistair Stewart and Lloyd Stinson were urged to run in Winnipeg South Centre and Winnipeg South. Along with David Orlikow and Stanley Knowles, the incumbent MPs for Winnipeg North and Winnipeg North Centre respectively, this would make an impressive slate.

SIDNEY GREEN

NDP leader Tommy Douglas was ready for the challenge facing his party. Political conviction, combined with political astuteness helped him to carve out positions on which the NDP stood alone. This included opposition to the stationing of nuclear weapons on Canadian soil. His position was strengthened by the fact that Pearson's government, in a mealy-mouthed turnabout, had pledged to accept nuclear weapons on Canadian soil – not because it was correct but because it honoured previously-made "commitments."

Since the Conservatives had torn themselves apart on this issue, Douglas was virtually alone among national party leaders to champion the cause. He could not and did not win the election, but the NDP vote held, with almost all of the former MPs re-elected.

There was no Liberal deluge. Instead Pearson only managed to form a minority government. In that House the Liberals held 129 seats, Conservatives 95, Social Credit 24, and NDP 17.

In addition to participating in the internal politics of the NDP, I was busier than ever in my law practice. Because of my association with Leon Mitchell, I was involved in numerous court cases in regard to the rights of trade unions. Several cases in the field of labour injunctions wound up in the Supreme Court of Canada.

I also became an active councillor. Metro government was an significant feature of Manitoba politics and some of my contributions helped carve out a political image. I was a proponent of keeping transit fares low and spoke of the possibility of eliminating them. My suggestions led to the adoption of a five-cent bus fare for people moving from one downtown location to another. The experiment was attempted on a trial basis, was discontinued and then became a regular feature in downtown Winnipeg in the 1970s and 80s. During the latter period buses operated at no charge.

The Metro chairman was appointed by the provincial government. I introduced a motion that the chairman be an elected councillor. Ultimately this plan was put into operation.

Steve Juba, the mayor of Winnipeg, had repeatedly called for the amalgamation of municipalities in Greater Winnipeg as a way to increase the efficiency of operation. I made a motion to that effect but it was defeated on a vote of six to four. I later introduced a similar resolution in the provincial legislature as an opposition member. That motion was also defeated. I continued to pursue the objective of the unification of Winnipeg and it ultimately occurred in 1971 when the NDP government created Unicity.

Other projects in which I was involved as a councillor included the purchase of river bank property with the objective of establishing a public park at the junction of the Red and Assiniboine Rivers. I argued that every child in school learned that Winnipeg was situated at the junction of these rivers but very few could see it because of the buildings and railway tracks blocking the view. In some parts of St. Boniface, one had a clear view at ground level but the site was virtually inaccessible.

I was also vocal in resisting bureaucratic urging to charge a fee to visit the Assiniboine Park Zoo. The policy of the zoo being open to all citizens at public rather than individual expense persisted long after my departure from council. The first fees for entry to the zoo were imposed on March 1, 1993.

In October 1964 I was narrowly re-elected in a contest where ethnic votes decided the issue. My main opponent, John Solimko, won among Slavic voters while I won with the support of traditional New Democrats and Jewish voters, most of whom I knew in the Garden City part of the constituency.

Many of my efforts at council received favourable comment, but probably the biggest story involved the zoo. When our family visited the zoo, I noticed the lioness was without a mate and appeared to be depressed and lonely. At the next Metro meeting I, not entirely tongue in cheek, raised the subject of cruelty to the lioness by depriving her of a male companion. The reaction was explosive. The story hit the front page, along with a picture of the lioness to demonstrate the validity of my grievance.

During my time on council, I formed some lasting relationships, particularly with Peter Taraska, a north-end Councillor who was of a diametrically opposite political persuasion, and a former classmate, Charles Huband, who had been elected to council shortly after I was. Huband subsequently became leader of the Liberal party in Manitoba and ultimately a judge in the Court of Appeal before whom I make frequent appearances.

In the summer of 1965, councillors and Chairman Bonnycastle enjoyed their annual golf tournament at the Kildonan Park Golf Course. During the social held that evening at the Bonnycastle residence, a news item was broadcast indicating that Prime Minister Pearson had asked for writs to be issued for an election to be held November 6, 1965.

The news created a serious problem for the NDP nationally and for me personally. Bonnycastle, who was intently watching my reaction to the news broadcast, correctly guessed that Metro was going to lose me to the federal election campaign. One could not simultaneously contest a federal election and hold a seat on Metro council.

Because I had been heavily involved in election matters as president of the provincial party, I felt that it was my responsibility to invest totally in the national fight. That meant running for office again in what would be a non-winnable seat of Winnipeg South.

1965 FEDERAL ELECTION

Prime Minister Lester Pearson called the 1965 federal election purportedly because he could not govern without a majority. Indeed during the campaign he publicly indicated that if the Canadian people failed to give the Liberals a majority, another election would be held. Such a rationale for calling the election was not credible because while Pearson had a minority government there was no suggestion that his program was in jeopardy.

His 1963 commitment to accept nuclear weapons on Canadian soil had been fulfilled and this was no longer an issue. However, it looked like the Liberals needed a majority, not so much to implement their policies, but rather to dodge implementation, particularly with regard to Medicare.

A national medicare program had been a major Liberal commitment in the previous election campaign and other parties expressed no serious opposition to its implementation. Indeed, Pearson was guaranteed the support of the NDP.

But while the Liberals were committed to medicare, constitutionally this subject was within the provincial jurisdiction. The government depended heavily on Quebec MPs, and Quebec jealously opposed the federal government being involved in any area of provincial jurisdiction. With a majority, the Prime Minister could water down his commitment.

The Liberal campaign attempted to eliminate the so-called fringe parties, namely the NDP and the Social Credit. As in previous federal elections the NDP viewed the contest as being critical to its continued strength and survival.

In Manitoba I, as party president, attempted to enlist a strong field of candidates. One new face was already on the slate when Ed Schreyer, who was the youngest person elected to the provincial legislature, decided to run in the federal riding of Brokenhead, a seat previously won and lost by his father-in-law, Jake Schultz.

I persuaded Rev. Philip Petursson, a respected Unitarian minister, to contest Winnipeg South Centre. As a result there was a powerful NDP Winnipeg slate consisting of incumbent MPs Stanley Knowles and Dave Orlikow, along with Petursson, Schreyer and Green.

As chairman of the party's provincial election campaign committee, I not only conducted a vigorous campaign in Winnipeg South, but was also active throughout the province, speaking and enlisting candidates.

During the campaign, NDP leader Douglas was magnificent as he attacked the Liberal government mercilessly in a series of public rallies throughout the country. He concentrated on medicare and the U.S. participation in the war of Vietnam. Again, he was the only national politician who gave objectors to the war somewhere to turn.

Douglas followed this path out of firm conviction and it was an effective political issue. Since the normal tendency of the electorate was to vote for or against the government, those voting against the government were apt to choose the party which was most likely to defeat the government, namely the Conservatives. To some extent, Douglas was able to swim against the tide by pursuing an issue which crossed party lines.

In Winnipeg South I campaigned against Liberal incumbent Margaret Konantz and Tory hopeful, broadcaster Bud Sherman, as if I were in the thick of the race. Public meetings were held and were reasonably well attended. My pamphlet carried the slogan "More people are voting for Green." It proved to be accurate.

Towards the end of the campaign Sherman publicly challenged Konantz to a public debate. With alacrity I, who had not been invited, publicly accepted the challenge. Newspapers printed Mrs. Konantz's refusal to participate but failed to mention my acceptance. This marked the beginning of a tactic that I would use throughout my political career. (This tactic will be explained in a separate chapter.)

Throughout the contest, I was assisted by my campaign manager, Una Decter, a south Winnipeg party activist who was to feature strongly in NDP activities and in particular, my future leadership bids. I chose her because she was the best person available, not because she was a woman. During this campaign, the feminist movement had not yet made sex a determining factor in selecting political persona.

My committee was innovative and even took advantage of Halloween night. Houses of NDP members throughout the constituency were given cardboard "apples" bearing the message "Green will be ripe on November 6." Thousands of children received these apples in addition to other treats. The apple story was unique enough to appear in the *Times of London*.

Meanwhile the Douglas election rally at the Winnipeg Auditorium attracted 5,000 people. Even the *Winnipeg Free Press* acknowledged that Orlikow and Knowles should be re-elected.

And they were re-elected. On November 8th the Canadian people gave Pearson the rebuke he deserved. The Liberals were re-elected with a minority government. The NDP held its own nationally, and in Manitoba gained an additional MP – Ed Schreyer.

I received 10,000 votes, more than had ever been obtained by the NDP in Winnipeg South. (In 1963, Stinson had received 8,000 votes.) Because Konantz lost to Sherman by less than 10,000 votes, she blamed her loss on me, claiming that I had drawn votes from the Liberals. I responded by saying that Mrs. Konantz caused my defeat. When asked "how", I said if the 20,000 who voted for Konantz had supported me, I would have won.

Some thirty years later my son, Marty, was examining the 1965 campaign literature and said to me, "Now I know why you lost the 1965 election." When asked to explain he noted, "The people in Winnipeg South realized that you don't know how to spell." Marty pointed out that running vertically along the side of the front page was printed "New Democractic Party." Approximately 30,000 pieces of this pamphlet had been distributed and it is reasonably safe to say that nobody noticed the misspelling.

Fortunately this error was not pointed out until thirty years later. It is the kind of nightmare that causes candidates to lose sleep. In an election campaign, the candidate is so egocentric that he believes his every word, action and thought is observed as though he was in a fish bowl. If only it were so. By and large the candidate's problem is that he is ignored. Most citizens who do not participate in the election know this full well. If the misspelling had been pointed out to me during the campaign, I would have viewed it as disastrous and would have tried desperately to figure out a way to counteract what I believed would get a negative reaction from voters. Thankfully I was spared such anxieties.

The best jibe of the election belonged to John Diefenbaker. During its 1963 - 65 term, the Pearson government had been riddled with a series of scandals. One involved a prisoner named Rivard who escaped after having been allowed by prison authorities to flood a skating rink. In one of his merciless attacks on petty corruptions, the Tory leader said that Pearson's decision to call an election in order to get a majority made the Prime Minister the first politician to run on the slogan "Throw the rascals in."

When the election ended, I was no longer an elected politician. I was however, more heavily involved in politics at the national and provincial levels than ever before. And now the overriding issue for the Manitoba NDP was the coming provincial election.

As president, my role in party affairs was magnified because provincial leader Russ Paulley and his caucus were relatively inactive in that area. I on the other hand, was heavily involved and that led to some of the difficulties I experienced in future years.

1966 PROVINCIAL ELECTION

After federal defeat, my political career as president of the party intensified. I became more involved with the organization of the provincial New Democratic Party.

Lloyd Stinson had nominated me for president. His speech was brief and to the point. "He is abrasive – he steps on toes – we need him." Party members agreed and I was elected with an overwhelming majority over Bob Murdoch, the incumbent president, and Ben Hanuschak, a close friend and colleague.

In assuming the presidency, I became heavily involved in party business which was largely devoted to fund raising and membership drives. Combined with building up to the next election, such activities were like being on a treadmill. The party had to walk very quickly merely to stay in the same place.

Fund-raising was intensified but revenue rarely exceeded the cost of paying the staff required to conduct the activities. A series of dinners honouring party stalwarts were moderately successful, with honorees such as Inkster MLA Morris Gray, former party leader Lloyd Stinson and the revered veteran MP Stanley Knowles.

The increased party activity had some liabilities as far as I was concerned. My work was generally appreciated and I gained approval and recognition throughout the province. Internally, however, I began to create enemies among those who regarded the party as a select group of people, whose role was to hold the "faith." In their view, they alone were blessed with the intellect to really appreciate the party ideology.

Shortly after the federal election, I received a visit from Stinson. The veteran was blunt. He suggested that I take over the leadership of the provincial party, a position held by Russ Paulley. I was flattered by the suggestion from such a respected New Democrat but said that there was lots of work to do for the party. I made no reference to the leadership question but did indicate my intention to run in the next provincial election. What would happen later remained to be seen. Stinson said he simply wanted me to know what he had in mind and the meeting ended.

Shortly thereafter, Inkster MLA Morris Gray, announced that he would not be running in the next provincial election which was expected in 1966. In party circles it was automatically assumed that I would be nominated. The "ward boss" of the Inkster constituency was Len Stevens, an official of the United Steelworkers of America. As one of the lawyers who handled steelworkers affairs, I was closely connected with him. When Stevens asked me to be the nominee I agreed.

I was not aware however that another United Steelworkers official, Howard Mitchell, also wanted the nomination for this supposedly safe NDP seat. With the help of Bill Puloski, a fellow union member, Mitchell ensured that a group of steel workers and other supporters were paid-up members and were present at the nomination meeting at Stevens' home.

When I arrived, I saw about thirty people present whom I had never met before. Since competition was totally unexpected I immediately realized that I was being led to slaughter. The vote was virtually unanimous and Mitchell became the NDP candidate for Inkster.

Disappointed but not bitter I decided to take an alternate path. I had been courted by people in the Osborne riding, part of my former federal area and I believed the constituency was winnable. With the good relationships I had established I was willing to face the challenge.

Then, without warning Steve Juba, the highly popular mayor of Winnipeg, announced that he was going to be a candidate in Inkster. He argued that the area was not an NDP constituency and the party only held it because of personal support for Gray. As far as Juba was concerned, it was now up for grabs and he intended to grab it.

Shortly after Juba's announcement, Mitchell decided to withdraw his candidacy citing health reasons.

Once again I was approached to seek the NDP nomination and run against Juba. I was reluctant to shift directions, but Stevens was adamant, assuring me that this time there would be no surprises. At a sparsely attended nominating meeting I became the official NDP candidate in the Inkster constituency and, within a short time Juba announced he would not be running.

During that period, I was still deeply involved in party activities. My presence was sought at meetings throughout Manitoba. Meanwhile the provincial executive, which now functioned as an election committee, met on a weekly basis. After intense efforts the party fielded 53 candidates, more than in any previous election, when the election was called by Premier Duff Roblin for June 23, 1966.

The Roblin government had problems which it did not wish to disclose. While the Premier prided himself on being a progressive – in contrast to his predecessor, Douglas Campbell who had the reputation of keeping a tight fist on provincial expenditures – Roblin's spending policy was starting to cause concern within his own cabinet.

The budget introduced in 1966 clearly demonstrated no adequate relationship between revenues and expenditures. Rumour spread that Roblin wanted to hold an election before he was forced to impose a sales tax in order to improve revenues.

I focused on that issue when, accompanied by Doug Rowland, NDP research assistant, I spoke at a Brandon constituency meeting. Referring to the budget, I compared Roblin to the Wizard of Oz who stood behind a screen and created illusions which had no relationship to what was happening. I said the illusions were created simply by the Wizard pulling levers and pushing buttons.

During the long drive back to Winnipeg, an enthused Rowland said I had just provided the budget response for the NDP caucus. Within days, Saul Cherniack made a speech in the legislature that largely mirrored what I had said in Brandon. The St. John's MLA received considerable news coverage for his 'Wizard of Osborne' address.

The 1966 election saw the New Democrats with an impressive array of new and credible candidates. They included Russ Doern in Elmwood, Sam Uskiw in Brokenhead, Ben Hanuschak in Burrows, Saul Miller in West Kildonan, Mike Kawchuk in Ethelbert Plains, Peter Fox in Kildonan and Philip Petursson in Wellington. These newcomers were all elected, as well as myself in Inkster. The margin of victory of 1,900 votes exceeded that of the previous NDP candidate.

As a result, at the age of 37, I became a member of the legislature and my political career reached a new threshold.

1966 NDP CAUCUS

The 1966 election marked a significant turning point for the Manitoba NDP. Its percentage of the popular vote increased from 14 to 26. The party ran more candidates than ever before and elected 11 members. And because the election in Churchill was delayed, it stood to gain another member and equal the number of Liberals elected.

The Churchill election was delayed for about two weeks because of weather. NDP strength was centered in Thompson and the backbone of the party organization was the United Steel Workers of America, the bargaining agent for the International Nickel Company miners.

The party nominee was Wilf Hudson, a respected union official. Invited to assist in the campaign, I spent several days in Thompson. My last suggestion before leaving related to sign publicity. I recommended that, on the night before the election, numerous signs be put up with the words "It's Hudson's Day" in order to have the greatest impact on people going to work or shopping in the morning.

Because the Liberal nominee had been late in filing nomination papers it was a two-man race between the Conservatives and the NDP. The Conservative candidate was the incumbent Gordon Beard, a popular hotel keeper in Thompson. He won, but Hudson received 40 per cent of the vote – enough to win in most three-man races.

The standing in the legislature was Conservatives 33, Liberals 12, NDP 11 and Social Credit 1. Most observers said the NDP had made the most important electoral breakthrough of that particlar contest.

In the years leading up to 1966, the Liberals were the acknowledged opposition while the NDP/CCF was the third party. During that time, the Russ Paulley/Saul Cherniack strategy had been to have the NDP function as the conscience of the legislature, above party politics and the acrimonious debates inspired by the Liberals against the government. New Democrats regarded the Liberals as the prime target and believed that displacing them as the official opposition would be the ultimate in political success.

Because of this philosophy they often criticized the Liberals and supported the government. Indeed, Cherniack was the darling of the Premier and most Tory cabinet ministers. The affection was reciprocated and he showed great respect for ministers including Attorney-General Sterling Lyon, Minister of Finance Gurney Evans, and Minister of Health Dr. George Johnson.

This traditional posture was to change dramatically after the 1966 election. The new caucus was not interested in being the conscience of the Legislature and instead concentrated attack on the government. The Liberals were virtually ignored. During throne speech and budget debates the NDP strategy was to introduce amendments to Liberal motions of non-confidence, which the Liberals could not possibly support.

One approach was to add a proposal to implement a public auto insurance program to a Liberal amendment. Inevitably, the Liberals and Conservatives would vote together to defeat the NDP's sub-amendment. It was the NDP caucus' strategy to do this as often as possible in the hope that, when the next election arrived, the public would recognize the New Democrats were the true opposition while the Liberals were allied with the government.

This approach was a radical change from the past and the NDP quickly began to get more media attention. Some veterans were uncomfortable with the new approach but any hesitation was swept away by the enthusiasm of the new caucus members.

They did not want the NDP to become the official opposition. They wanted to displace the government. This message was so powerful that it could not be resisted. Even Cherniack gave his half-hearted support although he regarded the goal as being totally unrealistic. He preferred the party to remain the conscience of the Legislature, rather than power hungry.

The media recognized that I was becoming one of the party's most promising new members and an effective debater. My first priority was to deal with collective bargaining, a subject which I had argued at all levels of the judiciary.

My thesis with respect to labour law is an important feature of my political history and deserves a brief comment. I had argued in the courts and in the political forum that it was a basic right of a worker to align himself with co-workers and use the combined strength as bargaining power for the purpose of obtaining better terms and conditions of employment.

I argued that any legislative infringement of this right constituted an attack on the principle of free collective bargaining. Thus, all statutes which pretended to legalize trade unions and set restrictions on when and how employees choose to utilize their bargaining power were a threat to the working man.

I used two examples to demonstrate my position. The courts had granted injunctions to stop the peaceful display of information by employees who had a dispute with their employer. I claimed that, since no other people were restricted from carrying signs expressing a non-slanderous position, no trade unionist should be treated differently.

I also noted that the courts and the legislatures in North America had adopted a habit of ordering people to work under the guise of stopping illegal strikes. Ordering a person to perform personal services was a concept foreign to the English common law. I maintained that a radical and discriminatory concept was being applied with respect to employees.

I had argued these positions in the courts on behalf of trade unions. In the legislature I proposed resolutions which would undo what the courts had been doing with respect to these concepts and to free collective bargaining generally.

In every case, I emphasized that I was not pursuing these positions on behalf of labour, but rather on behalf of the civil rights of every citizen. Freedom was indivisible, I argued, and if the state or the courts deny freedom to one person in society, it is a denial of freedom to all.

Those arguments impressed members of the legislature but the resolutions were not passed. They were dismissed, generally because they allegedly favoured labour over employers and would result in labour violence. That approach made me a favorite of the trade union movement in Manitoba and I held regular consultative meetings with union representatives.

In addition to dealing with labour issues, I argued NDP positions which did not involve the expenditure of public money. It was an attempt to dispel the notion that New Democrats were irresponsible spenders. For instance, I maintained a public auto insurance program would not cost the public money, but would rather save money – something which has become abundantly clear today during the post 9/11 insurance industry meltdown.

I also argued that all of the municipalities in greater Winnipeg should be unified in order to save public money.

When the Conservative government was dragged kicking and screaming into a national medical care program, Premier Walter Weir imposed a premium on all Manitoba families to finance the program, thus making it as unpalatable as possible.

I attacked the premiums and went on to demonstrate mathematically that either a sales tax or income tax would cost the average citizen far less than a premium. No public monies would be necessary to implement this measure because the same amount of monies would be collected and spent. The only change would be the way in which it was collected.

The Manitoba Development Fund ("Corporation" later under the NDP) was set up by the Roblin government to enable it to use public monies to finance private business. Those activities were totally secret. To me, this represented the final capitulation of the free enterprise system. In my view, the government knew the economy would fail without huge injections of public monies.

I maintained the government had chosen the worst of all possible options: the public would do the financing and, in the event of failure, lose its investment, while in the event of success the so-called captains of industry would get the reward normally earned by the investor and the government would get nothing.

The biggest bonanza which the Roblin government agreed to finance was a pulp mill at The Pas. The program was to be a $90 million investment in the Manitoba forestry industry. Documents leaked to Cherniack indicated that the project was actually being financed by the Manitoba Development Fund at a preferred interest rate. The minister responsible for the Fund refused to answer any questions about the matter because they related to private commercial business which would be sensitive to such questions. I argued that the use of public money required public disclosure. I will deal with this important subject in more detail later.

Public auto insurance, elimination of medicare premiums and reorganization of greater Winnipeg were all matters that did not involve the expenditure of money. To the contrary, effective implementation of these programs would result in the saving of money.

During 1967 and 1968 a race for leadership of the federal Conservative party was highlighted in the news. John Diefenbaker had been knifed in the back by the party establishment and numerous candidates for his position presented themselves. The most credible was Robert Stanfield, then premier of Nova Scotia. The name of Duff Roblin also surfaced but the Premier was officially negative to the idea.

Roblin was far more dynamic than the plodding Stanfield. He was also fluently bilingual, very important for a national leader in 1967. However he played hard to get. One evening during the 1967 legislative session, the Premier, Sterling Lyon, Saul Cherniack, Russ Paulley and I were enjoying a social drink in Roblin's office. The usual political friendly banter took place and this exchange occurred between Roblin and myself:

> Green: "Well, are you going for the big job?"
> Roblin: "What are you talking about?"
> Green: "You know darn well what I'm talking about."
> Roblin: "You mean the national leadership?"
> Green: "Of course."
> Roblin: "A man would have to be insane to go for that job."
> Green: "Well, that doesn't disqualify you."

One of Roblin's difficulties was his slow sense of humour. Ultimately he managed a forced smile but didn't really appreciate the lightness of the conversation. I used the story many times in my bid for leadership but made myself the butt of the joke by adding to the story "It didn't disqualify me either."

Roblin ultimately announced his candidacy for the federal leadership. He had support throughout the country and one of his trusted advisors was Maurice Arpin, a lawyer with whom I was relatively well acquainted and who advised Roblin on strategies effecting Franco-Manitobans and the relationship of Quebec to the rest of Canada.

Roblin, along with Stanfield and most Liberal cabinet ministers leaned towards what was then referred to as the 'deux nations' (two nations) concept. The concept was predicated on the proposition that Canada had two founding nations, one based on English-speaking people, who resided in all of the provinces with the exception of Quebec, and the other based on those of French origin, who were centred in Quebec.

The 'deux nations' concept emerged as a recognition that the Canadian constitution should provide particular status for the province of Quebec. As the home of most French Canadians, Quebec certainly was the centre of Canadian French culture even for those French-Canadians who lived outside of that province. John Diefenbaker was a vigorous opponent of the 'deux nations' concept and decided to fight for his position as national leader on the basis of his opposition to this program.

At the convention it became apparent that the final result would come down to a race between Roblin and Stanfield. Had it not been for his late entry into the race, Roblin would probably have succeeded, but Stanfield was chosen to be the national leader of the Progressive Conservatives by a very small margin.

Subsequently Roblin ran unsuccessfully in several federal elections and was eventually appointed to be a senator representing Manitoba. He is still highly regarded and recently authored a book which summarized his political career.

When Roblin resigned as premier, Manitoba was faced with a major political upheaval. Whoever was chosen as the new Conservative leader would automatically become the Premier. There were several candidates but it was generally thought that Roblin's most senior minister, Attorney General Sterling Lyon would be given the mantle of leadership. However Lyon, by his own abrasiveness, had made numerous enemies in the provincial party and in its caucus.

The rural members, in particular, wanted a dyed-in-the-wool Conservative to lead the party. Ultimately they chose Walter Weir, a long-time cabinet minister and representative of the rural constituency of Minnedosa. An amiable person, Weir was well-liked by all members of the Legislature but he did not appeal to youth or urban voters. He tried to gain political support by taking a negative attitude towards Quebec at federal-provincial meetings.

When the Legislature was called into session, the main item on the agenda was bringing Manitoba into the national medicare program which the federal government had instituted. Manitoba and Alberta in particular were adamantly opposed to the federal government using its spending powers to institute a national medicare program and acknowledged that they were coming into the program kicking and screaming. They were doing so only because the province would lose federal funding if they did not enter the program and would, at the same time, have citizens taxed for the provision of the program throughout the rest of the country.

Much of the beginning of the 1969 session involved debate over the method which the Conservatives had chosen to finance medicare. Indicating that he wanted citizens to be aware of the cost of the program, the premier decided to impose a premium which would apply equally to all citizens of Manitoba.

The New Democrats condemned this method of taxation and suggested that the program could be much better financed out of general revenues and taxes levied in accordance to the ability to pay rather than on a per capita basis.

Insofar as the NDP were concerned their political position was complicated by the leadership activities which were generated when I announced, in September 1968, that I would run for the leadership of the party.

PART TWO

CAMPAIGN FOR LEADERSHIP

1968 FEDERAL ELECTION

The 1968 federal election was a significant landmark in my career.

In 1965 Prime Minister Lester Pearson succeeded in attracting the so-called "three wise men" from Quebec. They were Jean Marchand, Gerard Pelletier and Pierre Elliot Trudeau. Luring them into the Liberal party was a significant coup because, while they were not members of the NDP, they were supporters. (Trudeau, a close friend of NDP vice-president Charles Taylor, had often appeared on the same platform supporting him.) After joining the Liberals, he was appointed Minister of Justice and developed a significant following among the Liberal left-wing in Canada.

When Pearson announced his retirement in 1968, there were numerous candidates for his position as leader and Prime Minister. The most prominent Liberal candidates were John Turner and Robert Winters but others such as Paul Hellyer and Judy LaMarsh also had aspirations.

Trudeau entered the contest late but his candidacy immediately caught fire. After several ballots, he emerged as winner, defeating Hellyer and Turner who had stayed in the race until almost the last ballot. After being installed as Prime Minister, Trudeau faced Parliament on April 23, 1968 and announced that a federal election would be held on June 25, 1968.

The Conservatives had also chosen a new leader. After a bitter fight, John Diefenbaker was dumped and Robert Stanfield, the distinguished Premier of Nova Scotia, defeated Duff Roblin on the final ballot. Stanfield was universally respected. More importantly he had a more positive attitude toward the problems of Quebec than Diefenbaker had demonstrated.

Not only had Stanfield acquired some capability in French, he also attracted support in Quebec by recognizing the fact that the province had a unique position in Confederation which should be recognized constitutionally. In fact, the concept of particular or special status was endorsed by all major political parties and most major candidates in the Liberal leadership race.

One notable exception was Trudeau. He stubbornly resisted any suggestion that the province of Quebec should be afforded special status. His position was simple: there were ten provinces in Canada and provincial powers enabled them to deal with their own distinct problems. Therefore Quebec had as much powers as it required in order to preserve its own identity.

Indeed, Trudeau was intellectually and politically opposed to any involvement by the federal government in areas deemed to be under provincial jurisdiction. If he had possessed the power, he would have opposed federal involvement in health and education. The Prime Minister told Ed Schreyer that, as far as he was concerned, the last social program in which Ottawa would get involved was Medicare.

Ironically Trudeau's position on Quebec was closer to the views expressed by Diefenbaker than it was to the Liberal policy. It was also very similar in its fundamental principles with the position subsequently adopted by Reform Party Leader Preston Manning.

During the 1968 election Trudeau attracted significant anti-Quebec support in the West as a Quebecer who would fight Quebec. While he had never said anything to justify this reaction, he must have known that it existed and certainly took advantage of it. By doing so, Trudeau succeeded in attracting western voters who were opposed to any special recognition of the distinct nature of Quebec.

Trudeau's position produced an ironic result in the election. The Conservatives and New Democrats had been dragged reluctantly into including in their platforms a position affording special status to the province of Quebec. Both Tommy Douglas and Robert Stanfield had adopted that position long after it had been tacitly accepted by the Liberals under Pearson and most of those who sought the leadership.

Trudeau stood alone on the special status issue and it paid handsome benefits. He won a majority government with significant representation from the western provinces. And because he was the only Quebecer with any real capacity to converse in French, he won overwhelming support in his own province from people who had no real concern about constitutional questions – as long as one of their own was Prime Minister.

The New Democrats managed to hold their own except for one important loss. Their leader Tommy Douglas – acknowledged to have been the best campaigner – lost a close race in B.C. to Liberal Ray Perrault. Although his opponent was of French origin, Douglas' defeat was almost certainly a consequence party's position on special status for Quebec. It did not have much support in B.C.

The New Democratic party was devastated. This was the second time that Douglas had failed to win his own seat. He continued to be adored and respected by New Democrats. He was also respected by most Canadians and his defeat was even a disappointment to many people who did not support the NDP. After all, he had been one of the most effective parliamentarians on the Canadian scene.

In late summer 1968, members of the federal NDP executive, including myself, met in Montreal. Douglas gave a report on the election and announced that he would not permit another member of Parliament to step aside so that he could run in a by-election. He had done this once before and felt guilty about snuffing out the political career of the man, Ernie Regier, who had stepped aside and precipitated a by-election which Douglas won. Nevertheless there was one small opening. If a by-election arose in the normal way, the leader would consider running.

When the meeting ended, the mood was glum. Everyone regretted Douglas' predicament but there did not appear to be any way out because his resolve was firm.

Several members went for a summer stroll on what had been the 1967 World Fair grounds on the island of Montreal. I was chatting with Alan Blakeney, a member of the executive, who subsequently became Premier of Saskatchewan. I told Blakeney that I intended to do something about the situation when I got back to Manitoba.

I was formulating an idea that could resolve the federal leader's problem. I knew there was growing dissatisfaction with the leadership of Russ Paulley. Federal MP David Orlikow and MLAs Saul Miller and Saul Cherniack had spoken actively about replacing him. Orlikow made several approaches to Ed Schreyer. Miller, who kept repeating the phrase "we can't go on like this", wanted Cherniack to run, while Cherniack played the role of an unwilling contender who would have to be dragged into the race.

False modesty is not one of my traits but I had no designs on the leadership. Besides, the manner in which I conducted himself as provincial president was not designed to win friends and influence people in regard to leadership. As Lloyd Stinson noted when nominating me as president I did 'step on toes.' Nevertheless, while I did not ingratiate myself with the veterans, I think I can say that I was held in esteem by many of my colleagues.

As for Schreyer being the way out of the dilemma, I was less enthusiastic than others, but regarded the youthful MP as a competent person who would make a very acceptable provincial leader – even though his views were more liberal than socialist. I was confident that my own influence in the party would overcome any ideological problems.

Therefore I formulated a plan which I believed would be acceptable at both the national and provincial levels. It involved Paulley stepping down, and Schreyer returning to Manitoba to become leader. This would create a by-election for Schreyer's former federal seat, where Douglas could run.

After returning to Winnipeg, I phoned Schreyer in Ottawa and told him what I had in mind. Schreyer seemed to be receptive. I then arranged a meeting with Paulley and Schreyer. We met for lunch at the Empire Hotel on Main Street in Winnipeg.

I reminded Paulley had that he always said that he would step aside if Schreyer wanted to seek the leadership. Paulley immediately confirmed that statement, but, waving his finger at me, added "and I will fight anyone else." I quickly assured him that I was not interested in a fight. I would support Schreyer. If Paulley did the same, Schreyer's leadership would be virtually acclaimed.

Russ Paulley was obviously stunned by the suggestion, but given his previous pronouncements, he could not conceivably object. He had never expected Schreyer would be willing to leave the national scene in order to lead a third-ranking party in Manitoba.

After pondering the situation, Paulley said he was in favour of the proposal but disagreed with the timing. This obviously indicated that Paulley opposed the suggestion in its entirety because timing was of the essence. It was necessary for two reasons: to get Douglas back on the national scene as quickly as possible and to ensure that a leadership change occurred in Manitoba before the next provincial election.

To my great disappointment, Schreyer immediately backed away and agreed with Paulley that while the idea was sound, implementation should be delayed. Neither one indicated what kind of delay was contemplated.

Totally unnerved, I left the meeting. What I thought was a perfect plan had been scuttled. Even worse, I believed it would be difficult for me to precipitate a leadership change in Manitoba since I had accepted Schreyer as a leader.

Within a few short weeks a tragic and unexpected event took place. Colin Cameron, a long time member of Parliament for the B.C. riding of

Cowichinaw on the Islands, died. It was virtually unanimous within the party that Douglas would contest the by-election. It was called quickly by the Prime Minister, Douglas won and returned to Parliament.

This, however, left the Manitoba party in a worse position than ever. Paulley remained the leader and despite his indication of resigning sometime in the future, he wanted to maintain the prestige, honour and salary which went along with that position.

I heard numerous complaints about the leadership and some members of the legislature prodded me to do something. On several occasions, MLA Peter Fox said I would have his support if I ran for leader.

Then Sam Uskiw phoned me to talk about a leadership change. When he said Al Mackling, a frequent candidate who had never won a provincial seat was being considered by some as a potential leader, it was the final straw. Although I recognized the problems if I sought the leadership, they did not relate to false modesty. I certainly believed I could do the job but also knew that I had stepped on so many toes in my organizational activities that I would not be accepted by many. Despite those misgivings, the possibility of serving under the leadership of Mackling, a man with dogmatic ideals for which I had little regard, was totally unacceptable.

I took matters in my own hands. In August I and Paul Kostas, a member of the Inkster executive, visited constituency president Len Stevens at Victoria Beach. I explained the situation and received Stevens' support to seek the leadership at the next provincial convention in November. At a meeting that evening the riding's executive also endorsed me.

I then phoned Russ Paulley. The conversation was brief. I told Paulley of my intentions and the leader acknowledged the information. I then called Ben Hanuschak and informed him of my decision. I did not lobby any of the members or seek to create a caucus support group even though many had indicated support in the past.

On September 3, 1968 I held a news conference at my law office to announce my plan to seek the party leadership. I said this was necessary because, if the party wished to be a contender in the next provincial election, it required a thorough review of all its positions, including the leadership.

At no time did I challenge the competence of Paulley as leader. I merely indicated that the leadership should be reviewed and that there should be a contest. My announcement took the party by storm. There were immediate calls of congratulations and support from many members. There were, however, no calls from any caucus colleagues.

On a television news program that announced my candidacy, Cherniack was asked about his intentions. His response was equivocal, indicating he was unsure what his position would be. Paulley merely referred to me as one of the most aggressive people that he knew.

Behind the scenes, Cherniack and Orlikow, egged on mainly by Miller, convened a meeting of caucus members. I was not invited. Prior to the meeting they had attempted to get Schreyer to commit himself to run for the leadership but he refused. However, he also refused to say that he would not do so. He left his own position completely open and gave others the opportunity to interpret his position as meaning what they wanted.

Miller and Cherniack tried to persuade the caucus that I was not the answer to the leadership problem. They did not defend Paulley and actually agreed that a change in leadership was necessary. However they were confident that while Schreyer had not committed himself, he would do so if presented with a unanimous call. If the caucus were united in rejecting my candidacy, they believed that Paulley would soon retire. In effect, they wanted to wait until Schreyer was ready.

The caucus then issued a statement on October 4, 1968 which read as follows:

> "Russ Paulley has led the New Democratic Party in Manitoba since 1961, and has gained the respect of members of the Party and of the citizens of Manitoba. He has been able to weld together a solid and effective Legislative team capable of directing the Government of the Province. He has indicated that no man is leader by Divine Right, and it is his intention to step aside for a successor acceptable to the Party who would lead it in its forward march. We recognize his great service to the Party and the people of Manitoba.
>
> We look for a leader with experience, with knowledge and with an understanding of, and an appeal to, all segments of Manitoba. A leader must be persuasive in presenting his opinion, but have the flexibility to reflect the point of view of the Caucus and all groups in our society who support the New Democratic Policy.
>
> Sidney Green, by his decision to challenge the leadership next month, has attempted to precipitate the issue now – without giving the members of the New Democratic Party sufficient time and opportunity to assess the possibilities of making the best choice of a successor to Paulley.
>
> We do not believe that the change must be made precipitously and want the necessary time to make certain that the best potential leaders are assessed and canvassed so that a convention will have a choice of several candidates and not be stampeded into a decision within a matter of weeks.
>
> At this time we favour Ed Schreyer, MP. He appears to have the best attributes for leadership within the Party and in the eyes of the

electorate. We are confident that Schreyer is sufficiently responsive to Party; needs to accept a draft and sacrifice all that it entails, but we cannot bring this about immediately. We are organizing a genuine "DRAFT SCHREYER" campaign for 1969.

We believe that whenever Premier Weir calls an election, the Party will be ready and able to assume the responsibility of Government."

This statement was issued by, and on behalf of, the following MLA's: Saul Cherniack, St. Johns; Russell Doern, Elmwood; Peter Fox, Kildonan; Lem Harris, Logan; Mike Kawchuk, Ethelbert Plains; Saul Miller, Seven Oaks; Philip Petursson, Wellington; Sam Uskiw, Brokenhead."

(Wednesdays are Cabinet Days, Russell DOERN, p.40)

The statement was allegedly supported by all members of the caucus with the exception of myself and Paulley. Indeed it was signed by all members except Hanuschak. It was Ben's way to be silent and while Cherniack and Miller interpreted his silence as acquiescence, Hanuschak quickly disabused them of that belief by not signing the caucus declaration. He also indicated that he would support me in the leadership race.

The caucus' statement repudiated Paulley as the leader – something I had never done. I indicated and still said that I was prepared to serve under Paulley. The eight who signed the declaration indicated that they did not regard Paulley as a suitable leader and made it clear that Schreyer, who was not running, should be chosen.

The statement undoubtedly gave the impression that those who signed did not wish me to be leader. This was a legitimate interpretation and those who had no such intention, such as Sam Uskiw, Peter Fox, Russ Doern, Pete Kawchuk and Philip Petursson, could not excuse themselves. Most of them had urged me to run for the leadership.

Following the caucus statement the media asked me whether I intended to reconsider my position. I responded with an emphatic "No." In fact I said the caucus had taken a position far more extreme than I had taken with respect to Paulley's capacity to lead.

The statement confirmed the desire for change. It did not question my assessment that a leadership review was necessary. The only thing questioned was the timing. The issue became one of "now" versus "sometime in the future." This issue became the basis of my campaign. Although I entered the leadership contest on the basis that the 'New Democratic Party was ready to govern', a slogan which had admittedly been plagiarized from Doern, my new campaign slogan was one simple word – "NOW."

That slogan deserves comment. In Alberta, the Social Credit party had been in power for almost two decades, while the Conservative party never got off the ground. Then Peter Lougheed, a prominent lawyer and a former Edmonton Eskimo football player, became the dynamic new leader of the Conservatives. In his campaign for the leadership which occurred after my first run, Lougheed's slogan was "NOW." Political pundits deemed the slogan to be a mark of genius after Lougheed won the leadership and ultimately the Premiership of Alberta. This was a perfect example of the proposition that success determines the quality of the slogan, rather than the slogan creating the success.

Following the caucus statement I held a press conference accompanied by 35 energetic supporters. At the press conference I disclosed the fact that I had met with Schreyer and Paulley and proposed that Schreyer become leader. I also stated that, because Paulley had questioned the appropriateness of the time, Schreyer had backed away. Since I regarded time to be of the essence I said Schreyer's position was not an acceptable way to resolve the problem. Accordingly, I suggested that if the reluctant MP was a candidate, the entire question could be resolved.

Several caucus members did attempt to urge Schreyer to actively contest the leadership in order to stop me but Schreyer, whose nature is to avoid confrontation if possible, refused. Instead he said that in order to have him run for leader in the future, the caucus would have to stop me in November. There was no choice but to follow that advice and opponents Miller, Cherniack and Orlikow fought much harder to prevent me from becoming leader than they ever fought to secure their own election.

The 1968 NDP leadership campaign was probably like no other campaign experienced by any political party.

The champions and organizers of Russ Paulley's campaign were led by my north-end colleagues Saul Cherniack, Saul Miller and David Orlikow. They had been the most active in trying to get rid of Paulley. In order to achieve this goal they had to take the position that they were not supporting Paulley but rather supporting Schreyer, who was not a candidate. Accordingly Paulley had to endure the humiliation of a leader campaigning on the basis that he was not fit for leadership.

I had expected some coldness or possible neutrality on the part of most of my colleagues. I was totally unable to predict that this group of experienced politicians would take the position that they were not prepared for a change – even though the leader was incompetent – until a third person, who was not a candidate, decided to participate.

Cherniack disclaimed any interest in the leadership but his disclaimer could not be taken seriously. On the day I announced my candidacy, Cherniack phoned Doug Rowland, his former research advisor who was now working with the federal caucus.

The conversation as reported to me by Rowland went as follows:

Cherniack: "I suppose you heard that Green has announced
for the leadership."
Rowland: "Yes."
Cherniack: "What do you think about it?"
Rowland: "Schreyer would be better."
Cherniack: "What about me?"
Rowland: "You can't do it."

Heeding that advice, Cherniack abandoned any notion of running himself, which is what Saul Miller was urging, and adopted the Schreyer strategy as a means of stopping me.

The extent that the Miller, Cherniack, Orlikow troika was willing to go in order to stop me is exemplified by a conversation which took place between Herb Schultz, Schreyer's brother-in-law, and Sybil Cherniack, Saul's wife. Schultz, who supported me, phoned the Cherniack residence. He asked Mrs. Cherniack why her husband was trying to prevent me from becoming leader, thereby retaining Paulley whom the Cherniack's regularly disparaged. She responded "He is a city lawyer and a Jew, and that's why Saul's not running."

Being a Jew and its consequences had always been a feature of my life. As a youngster I had been very self-conscious and sensitive to harassment by school mates and others. As I grew older I realized that it was the attackers who had a problem, not me. In fact people had elevated me to numerous positions in politics and other areas of public life with full knowledge that I was Jewish. I believed my Jewishness was not an impediment but rather – if anything – an asset. In my Inkster riding, which contained very few Jews, I was elected overwhelmingly, defeating Ukrainian and other more ethnically acceptable candidates. I found out that anti-semitism, such as existed, was not an impediment to my own journey to success.

Having conquered any sense of inferiority with respect to Gentile anti-semitism, I was totally unprepared for the phenonemon of Jewish fueled anti-semitism which I now encountered. Indeed Miller, Cherniack and Orlikow were all Jews who recognized my achievements in the party and my popularity throughout the province. Therefore they calculated that the only attack that could defeat me was a suggestion that people in Manitoba, particularly in rural Manitoba, would never elect a city Jewish lawyer. That became the lynch pin of the anti-Green campaign.

Whereas many non-Jews in the party would have been embarrassed and ashamed to conduct a campaign on this basis, they lost some of their timidity when the issue was raised by three prominent Jews.

The fact that the trio came from my home territory in Winnipeg North was even more significant. Cherniack and Orlikow acknowledged that my activity and organization in the area had helped the party and their own candidacies. I was tireless in organizational campaigns, far outdistancing more veteran colleagues. Now those who had been the beneficiaries of many of my activities were my main foes.

Orlikow in particular was relentless as he bad-mouthed me to everybody who would listen and some who did not want to listen. Len Stevens, the president of Inkster constituency, became so annoyed that he threatened to run against Orlikow for his Parliamentary seat.

Despite their efforts the anti-Green forces were unable to stem support for me from various parts of the province. The steelworkers in Thompson, where I had been a frequent speaker, announced their support. So did many people in rural Manitoba, particularly in the Gilbert Plains area where Herb Schultz had been raised. Many young people who had not been active in the party also climbed on the Green bandwagon, much to the chagrin of those, notably Miller, who claimed that I was too radical to attract liberal-minded people to the party. It was evident that the younger liberally-minded people did support me, while the old diehards stayed with Paulley.

The strategy of the Paulley forces was to underplay the fact that a serious leadership campaign was underway. They continued to harp on the fact that I could not get along with the caucus, a total falsity but which had gained credibility because of a signed statement. Indeed those who signed the statement began to get fidgety because they had created a situation where all of them could be defeated by a man who had only the support of Ben Hanuschak.

Before the convention, Paulley and I spoke at meetings throughout the province. On the whole they were poorly attended but support tended to favour me.

As the campaign proceeded the 'city-lawyer Jew' tactic seemed to be failing. Therefore the Paulley group accused me of causing dissension within the party and predicted that, if I were elected, it would go against the wishes of the people and lead to an irreparable rupture in party relations. That theme continued until the end.

At the convention I, as president, and Paulley, as leader, delivered reports which were for the most part unemotional, factual, and unprovocative. Resolutions were debated in the normal way with Schreyer participating. Delegates who wanted Schreyer as leader tried desperately to get him to change his position but he adamantly refused. But he did throw out a suggestion: if Paulley were elected, he would participate in the next leadership campaign.

The major part of the convention took place at the Convention Centre. The important issue that was discussed was a resolution calling for a unification of Greater Winnipeg. This position was largely supported by provincial and Winnipeg delegates. It was vigorously opposed by Saul Miller and Al Mackling, both of whom had served on municipal councils. When the resolution came to a vote, it was overwhelmingly passed. I subsequently introduced that resolution in the legislature. It constituted NDP policy as confirmed by a convention. This fact had some significance in view of what took place after Schreyer was elected.

The actual leadership vote took place at the Fort Garry Hotel. When the party wanted Stanley Knowles to be the convention chairman he approached me and Paulley and said that he intended to behave as if he was the Speaker of the House. That meant if there was a tie vote, which was within the realm of possibility, he would do as a Speaker would do: He would rule that since there was no positive vote, the status quo would remain.

He asked for approval of this suggestion. Paulley approved. I did not. This was not a resolution, this was an election between two people and Knowles, as a delegate, had a responsibility to vote one way or another. Since Knowles did not wish to make a public vote, he decided not to act as chairman. As a result Cliff Scotten, the national secretary of the NDP, was asked to chair the meeting.

As the leadership contest began, the hall took on a different appearance. In the past, demonstrations, signs and other paraphernalia were absent since no real leadership race had been held in recent history. This time one set of signs proclaimed "Paulley for unity." Other signs consisted of a green background with the word NOW across the centre of it with the message intended to be "Green Now." The campaign buttons also made no reference to the candidate's name. They were simply green and became known as the 'green button'. In addition, many of the Green delegates wore green attire. Based on the signs it was apparent that the vote would be close.

I was nominated by Herb Schultz. He stressed the fact that Schreyer was not a candidate, there was no guarantee that he would become a candidate and the only candidates were Green and Paulley. He then praised my achievements outlining what had happened to the party since I began to take an active role.

In his nominating speech for Paulley, Cherniack reiterated the MLAs' position and made hypocritical remarks about the candidate's qualities as a leader. The remarks were at total variance to the opinions expressed by him and his colleagues for several years.

In my speech I gave a short history of the NDP's practice of voting on the leadership at every convention. Other parties did not. I said it was my naive belief that those who maintained that the concept of a leadership contest was a perfectly normal procedure for which nobody should be criticized, really meant what they said.

I told the story of a meeting where one participant kept saying, "Throw him out." After he had said this several times another member said, "But he's not here." The response was, "Then bring him in and throw him out." I believed that was happening to me. I was being criticized for doing what the party had continually professed was an admirable thing.

I dealt with the question of my loyalty to the party. Many things had been said about me during the campaign but the most praiseworthy was being said in the hall by the Paulley supporters. Pointing to the Paulley signs bearing the words, "Paulley for unity", I maintained the message of the signs was that my supporters were so dedicated and loyal that if Paulley was elected, they would rally round the leader and there would be unity in the party. Presumably, I added, the loyal Paulley supporters would also accept a decision of a majority with respect to the leadership. My supporters responded with enthusiastic applause.

I went on to say that the only question facing the delegates was not whether new leadership was needed. It was whether the change should be done immediately or at some undetermined time. I reminded delegates that a provincial election was coming and if they wanted a leadership change, now was the time. I advised them not to run the risk of not having a change when the election is called and the campaign is conducted by a person who had been discredited by his own supporters.

In closing I quoted Shakespeare, "There is a tide in the affairs of men when taken at the flood leads on to fortune. Omitted, all the voyage of their lives is drowned in sorrows and in misery. On such a full sea are we now afloat and we must take the current when it serves or lose our venture." The speech was warmly received.

Then Paulley spoke. He was in good form, as he always was when engaged in a fight. The main thrust of his speech focussed on the progress between 1965 and 1968 – the period during which I was the president of the party.

Paulley took out the newspaper headlines which appeared after the 1966 election. They were perfect campaign literature for him. The *Free Press* printed a picture of an exuberant Paulley accompanying the story that the NDP was the only victor in the race.

When the leadership vote was completed, Paulley received 216 votes as compared to 178 votes for me. A 20-vote shift would have given me the leadership.

During a TV interview that night Paulley and I were very cordial to each other. I took the position that the NDP would be led by Paulley into the next election. Paulley, who attempted to shed the impression that he was merely holding the fort until Schreyer was ready, said he would assume full leadership and responsibilities for the party for the indefinite future.

1968/69 LEGISLATIVE SESSION

Major issues were discussed during the 1968/69 legislative session. At the same time, behind the scenes and between the lines the NDP leadership question was percolating. Those who had supported Russ Paulley now abandoned him and began frantic manoeuvres to get him to stand aside and make room for Ed Schreyer.

In early 1969, four by-elections were held in the ridings of Emerson, Churchill, Wolseley and Birtle-Russell. They were make-or-break contests for the Liberal party. When Duff Roblin was premier, Liberal Leader Gil Molgat had never been able to crack through the Conservative wall. But when Roblin resigned to run unsuccessfully for the federal Conservative leadership, provincial Tories elected Walter Weir as leader. He was a likeable rural MLA, but did not appear to have the strength exhibited by Roblin or Sterling Lyon.

The four by-elections resulted in three victories for the Conservatives and one for the NDP. Joe Borowski won in the Churchill riding by a mere seven votes over a popular Thompson doctor, Blaine Johnstone, who ran for the Tories.

A well known populist in Manitoba, Borowski had gained tremendous press coverage when he set up camp outside the Legislative Building to protest against the provincial sales tax. He was regarded as a radical but had very conservative ideas about life, a fact which would become apparent after he was appointed a cabinet minister in the Schreyer government.

Because the win was so narrow, a recount was automatic. I was called to Thompson to act as Borowski's lawyer at the proceedings held before a county court judge. In a recount the role of the judge is to examine each ballot individually and the parties have the right to argue about rejection or acceptance of any ballot.

One of the first ballots to be considered had an "X" in the Borowski box and a very slight pencil mark in another location. The returning officer had rejected this ballot even though it appeared to carry a plain intention to vote for Borowski. I offered only a mild objection to the rejection of this ballot and the counting continued until noon.

At lunch Borowski ordered Southern Comfort and Coke and voiced his annoyance that a more vigorous pitch had not been made to include the ballot as a vote for him. It seemed that Borowski suspected me of not really representing his interests. This was quite consistent of the candidate's distrust of others. I quickly explained to Borowski that it was in Borowski's interest to maintain the status quo – a seven-vote lead. If the status quo was maintained in spite of rejecting this one ballot, I predicted Borowski would win. If the status quo is altered, that alteration could favour Johnstone. I didn't know how many ballots yet to be considered had favoured the other candidate but were rejected for the same reason.

Shortly after resuming a rejected ballot with a plain "X" after Johnstone's name but a slight pencil mark in another area, was considered. Using the precedent of the rejected Borowski ballot there was little room for argument by Johnstone supporters and the ballot remained rejected. As time passed, several other ballots were not included for the same reason and Borowski smiled at me with a knowing look. Those ballots were not included for the final count.

Following the re-count Borowski was declared elected. When he took his seat in the Manitoba legislature, the NDP had twelve members – the same number as the Liberals. It was the first time that the New Democrats were entitled to call themselves the second party in the House, albeit a tie.

When the Legislature met, Borowski immediately made the headlines by comparing the Conservative plan to flood South Indian Lake to the Auschwitz death camps. It was a rather extravagant comparison but was characteristic of a Borowski attack. It found favour with many New Democrats and he soon became one of the most popular members.

Once again the issues that received the most prominence were medicare premiums, public automobile insurance and the flooding of South Indian Lake. As well I introduced a resolution calling for unification of Greater Winnipeg. This embarrassed the Liberals since one of their candidates, Charles Huband, had espoused a similar policy but Molgat could not pursue it due to the opposition by some of his suburban members. Saul Miller also did not support it and Molgat moved an amendment calling for a referendum on the question. The resolution was ultimately defeated.

In the area of medicare premiums, the Conservative government had been dragged unwillingly into medicare and imposed an onerous premium on Manitobans, who were required by law to participate in the plan. I said the plan should be financed out of general revenues and not out of premiums.

The enactment of the medical insurance program paid by premiums could have had an unforeseen and damaging result to employees whose contract required the employer to pay the existing medicare premiums. Without some stipulation in the legislation the employees would lose this benefit and be required to pay the public premiums. Their employer would receive the full benefit of the legislation. This applied to the International Nickel Company in Thompson an and other employers.

I brought this to the attention of the legislature and argued forcibly that a stipulation should be put into the legislation which would remedy this situation so that the employee would continue to receive the benefits bargained for in the collective agreement. With some alterations the government accepted my argument and made an appropriate amendment to the legislation protecting the rights of the employer. Commenting on this, in her "Under the Dome" column, Ellen Simmons wrote (Winnipeg Free Press, April 3, 1969):

> "Medicare: Sidney Green wins Highest Praise from those without bias.
>
> ...That this proviso (that employers who have been paying hospital and/or medical care premiums for their employees as a fringe benefit included in a negotiated contract, shall, with the lower cost of medicare, continue to give their employees the same dollar benefit as before) is now in the bill, should make the NDP's Sidney Green a very happy man, for it was entirely his doing. Mr. Green, who is a lawyer with wide labour relations experience, spotted what failure to write this point into the act would mean (in the case of a large company like the International Nickel Company for example, which has over 6000 employees, it could mean in the neighbourhood of a quarter-million dollars). He argued the case with such vigor and clarity that, subsequent to hasty last-minute conferences among the ministers of health and labour and the legislative counsel, Health Minister George Johnson introduced an amendment to accomplish what Mr. Green asked for.
>
> Mr. Green in fact, has had a thoroughly good session. It is not often that a member of the opposition, by sheer force of persuasion and logic causes a government to rewrite legislation that is already in print: Mr. Green accomplished it. And he is the same man who, a few weeks ago, brought education minister Don Craik to heel on the matter of permitting treaty Indians to elect and be elected to school division boards ..."

I also took the major role in calling for the government to implement an automobile insurance program, a longstanding item in the NDP platform which had been implemented by Tommy Douglas in Saskatchewan.

The South Indian Lake issue was raised in the legislature by Liberal MLA Gordon Johnstone. Manitoba Hydro's Nelson River development program involved a diversion which would require the relocation of an Indian community situated at South Indian Lake. I had obtained details of this program from Dr. Cass Booy and Dr. Robert Newbury, professors at the University of Manitoba.

I quickly took the initiative on the issue and launched major attacks on the government in regard to its handling of the program. The government had decided to issue a licence even before the program had been approved and prior to the public hearings, which the Tories had instituted.

Meanwhile the leadership problem within the NDP surfaced on several occasions. At the opening of the session, I was elected as party whip. This was intended as an apology by colleagues for the suggestion, heard often during the leadership race, that I did not have their respect.

Paulley, however, was less conciliatory. While in Thompson in regard to the Borowski campaign, he reportedly told Brian Koshul of the steelworkers' union that he intended to stop Green from being the leader because the Jews were already running Winnipeg and he could not have them running the Province of Manitoba.

A more bizarre antic occurred during the debate on South Indian Lake. As the party spokesman on the subject, I had made what many considered a devastating attack on Tory minister Harry Enns during debate on spending estimates.

On the same day, in an obvious attempt to divert press coverage from my speech, Paulley got up and reiterated some of the criticisms made by me. Because legislative reporters normally report a party leader's speech, Paulley fully expected that his comments would preclude other coverage on the issue. However the next day, March 21, 1969, the *Free Press* did a most unusual thing. On the front page, in separate news stories it gave coverage to the speeches by both Paulley and myself.

The South Indian Lake issue continued to form a daily part of the legislative activities. Cherniack had learned that a study entitled "Transition in the North" had been prepared by Ralph Hedlin (of Hedlin, Menzies and Associates) but the Conservatives had not made it public.

Cherniack requested the study on several occasions and even suggested that, if the contents of the report were made public, New Democrats would support the government's legislation in regard to compensation for those forced to move from South Indian Lake. That commitment was totally contrary to the caucus position and had not been discussed. It was immediately repudiated by the caucus.

Meanwhile it became apparent to most political observers, and particularly those in the NDP, that Weir was planning to call a spring or summer election. This left Paulley supporters in somewhat of a panic. In November they had told the party it was safe to elect Paulley because there would be no election in the near future. Now their position was in great jeopardy.

Toward the end of the session Paulley was hospitalized. Cherniack, Miller, Sam Uskiw and David Orlikow went to see him and asked him whether he would resign. That would provide sufficient time before the next general election for a leadership convention and Schreyer could become the leader. To their amazement Paulley refused. He intended to stay on. This put Cherniack, Miller and Orlikow in such a panic they told Paulley that if he continued to take that position Green would be elected leader. That was too much for Paulley. He immediately indicated that he would resign as leader of the NDP. He did so on his return to the legislature on April 30, 1969.

On the same day the press interviewed me and I indicated my intention to be a candidate for leadership. Within a few days Schreyer was persuaded to run. Before announcing his candidacy, he visited me at my home. Very apologetic, he sought to avoid confrontation and we had a pleasant conversation. Schreyer indicated that his colleagues had convinced him to run and that it would be a civilized campaign. He also said that if at any stage he got the impression that I would receive as much as 40 per cent of the vote – which I had received in the previous campaign – he would withdraw. I immediately rejected the suggestion. I indicated that the leadership problem in the NDP would not go away if I was elected on the basis that Schreyer was not present. For me, leadership could only mean something if I was successful running against Schreyer. If that did not occur and Schreyer became leader, I would accept the result.

Many people have over-emphasized the policy differences between myself and Ed Schreyer. Actually, Schreyer was more of a populist than I was. He wanted to help the average person and was very comfortable when associating with what would be colloquially referred to as the ordinary guy. My own ideas were probably more intellectually-oriented. But our policy differences were not major ones and Schreyer would easily accept my policy recommendations if he thought they would be readily supported. The real difference comes down to this: Schreyer was a man who believed that everything could be worked out and conciliated. I was a man who believed that everything had to be thought out and fought out if they were to result in meaningful change.

The next day Schreyer held a news conference, announcing his decision to run for the leadership. In making his announcement he referred to me as a "classical socialist" and described himself as a social democrat. When informed by the press of Schreyer's reference to me as a classical socialist, I said that I had never been insulted by being referred to as a socialist, but it would be an insult if I was referred to as a liberal.

The race was on.

LEADERSHIP, PHASE TWO

The legislature was still in session when Russ Paulley announced his resignation and Schreyer and I declared our candidacy for the NDP leadership. At the same time, general election fever was in the air as everyone believed that Manitobans would be at the polls by summer 1969.

In the House, debate on South Indian Lake remained a hot issue. On the morning of May 22, 1969 the Public Utilities Committee was meeting to consider a bill related to compensation for South Indian Lake residents and hear presentations from civil servants.

When one of the civil servants, Mr. George S. Bowman, concluded, MLAs were entitled to question him. When my turn came I asked whether some of the opinions and facts just expressed came from the report "Transition in the North." That report, which had not yet been made public, probably gained more prominence because of its secrecy than its actual contents. In any case, the civil servant responded in the affirmative. That led me to ask, "Will you then read the report to us?" The question was greeted with a stunned silence. The Chairman and Conservative MLAs objected. Adamantly I maintained that, if the witness' testimony had been based in part or in whole on the report, the Committee was entitled to know its contents.

By this time the noon break had arrived and the Committee adjourned until the afternoon. I went to the University of Manitoba Law School, where I was a lecturer in labour law. When I returned, I was advised that the writs had been issued and an election would be held on June 25.

The NDP was in a frantic state. The leader had resigned. An election had been called and no new leader had been chosen. I believed Paulley should continue leading the party. I maintained that holding a leadership campaign during the election campaign was unprecedented and could be potentially damaging. The Schreyer forces – as distinct from Schreyer himself – wanted the contest to take place. They could not face the party after promising there would be a new leader before the next election. They were willing to risk the problems associated with such a move in order to preserve their own hides.

Fortunately for the party, Schreyer and I conducted a campaign in, what most observers acknowledged to be, a totally civilized manner. We agreed to campaign in a series of joint public meetings held throughout the province.

The convention itself was scheduled for Saturday, June 7, 1969. That day was important because the deadline for Provincial nominations was June 11, 1969. Schreyer had advised the party quite frankly that if he was not elected as leader he had no intention of returning to Manitoba and would remain an MP. Therefore the leadership issue had to settled before the nomination deadline.

The first joint campaign meeting was held in the Beausejour area, Schreyer's home territory. Still smarting from Schreyer's reference to me as a "classical socialist", I began my address by focusing on issues he had dealt with in the Manitoba Legislature. They included Medicare premiums, unification of Greater Winnipeg, the flooding of South Indian Lake, and public automobile insurance. I then told the audience that every time I raised one of these issues, Sterling Lyon referred to me as a "classical socialist" or "radical socialist" and thought that epitaph would answer all arguments and end the debate.

I stressed to the audience – and more importantly to Schreyer – that the word "socialist" was not an answer to any argument and Schreyer would have to deal with provincial issues which, up to this point, he had not done.

Schreyer had entered the campaign basically because Premier Walter Weir had made a bad impression in Ottawa. Initially Schreyer did not deal with any provincial issues that had been discussed in the Legislature. As a matter of fact, he had some doubts about the NDP opposition to The Pas Forestry complex and its approach to the South Indian Lake issue. Over the course of the campaign however, Schreyer gradually adopted every position the Manitoba caucus had expounded in the Legislature.

We were in a contest, but a certain rapport developed between us as a result of our close association during the campaign. We conversed in French, German and English as we discussed various issues. While driving from Thompson to Flin Flon with Joe Borowski, we discussed the school aid question. I was adamantly opposed to any public funding for private schools. Schreyer was in favour of some funding. Borowski was also in favour of some funding and Schreyer undoubtedly thought that, because of their agreement on this issue, he had gained the support of one of Manitoba's most popular MLAs. He was to learn that Borowski was not as simplistic a personality as some had been led to believe.

The NDP leadership race seemed to overshadow the election campaign with extensive media coverage of both candidates. There were almost daily reports of the leadership delegates and the positions taken – which were essentially anti-Conservative rather than personal attacks.

Press reports also indicated that Schreyer was far from a "shoo-in." As a matter of fact, an announcement of support for me from 29 university professors came as a shock to the media as well as the Schreyer forces. Many of Schreyer's supporters, particularly Orlikow, Cherniack and Miller could not believe that with Schreyer in the race people would continue to support his opponent – despite the fact that at most meetings I was making the more interesting and crowd pleasing addresses.

As the campaign progressed Schreyer began to use part of his speech to make laudatory remarks about his opponent. At one meeting he acknowledged that I was one of the most effective parliamentarians that he knew and would be a member of his cabinet if he became the Premier of Manitoba.

I restrained himself from making the suggestion that I would like to say the same thing about my rival but Schreyer would not be coming to Manitoba unless he was the leader. It was in keeping with my determination not to create any bad impressions insofar as Schreyer was concerned.

In the meantime the public image campaign in Winnipeg was progressing favourably insofar as I was concerned. While Schreyer promoters claimed that their candidate would attract new intellectual and liberal-minded people to the party, there were indications that this group favoured me. The group of twenty-nine university professors announced their support for me.

Then, on June 3, 1969, five young Liberals, including Jay Kaufman, Paul Barber, Shalom Schacter, Jim Carr and Cliff Shnier announced their defection from their party and their support for the NDP and for my candidacy. That put Schreyer forces in a panic.

When Miller was approached about this development, he suggested that the young Liberals had a secret plot to help destroy the NDP by getting me elected as leader. The fact that the five had indicated that they would continue to stay with the NDP if Schreyer was elected, was ignored. It was a strange position for a New Democrat to take, but Miller's hostility to me and my achievements caused him to abandon all restraint in making pronouncements designed to hurt me.

On the surface, I appeared to be winning the media campaign, but it became apparent that the public perception was not reflected at the delegate level. The Schreyer people had the upper hand even if they didn't know it.

The nub of the situation is best demonstrated by what occurred at the North Winnipeg meeting on May 22, 1969 where both candidates made presentations. That area was my stomping ground and a large enthusiastic audience was present at the Hebrew Sick Benefit hall to hear what the candidates had to say. I appeared to have the upper hand in terms of audience approval.

Following the two speeches, Al Mackling posed a question to be answered by both candidates. He asked each one to indicate what he considered to be the best feature of his opponent. Schreyer responded with a very laudatory statement about me, which was at the same time cleverly self serving. He indicated that he had been to the Provincial Legislature, the House of Commons, the United Nations and several other bodies of national or international importance and had never heard anyone more clearly explain a difficult concept and make it understood than I had done.

I answered Mackling's question with a concise response: "He's a winner." In effect, my answer was the nub of the election campaign. New Democrats now wanted a winner. They had caught the fever of my campaign slogan "Ready to Govern." They wanted to govern and perceived that, regardless of individual competence, Schreyer had a better chance of winning support throughout Manitoba.

Another factor was that, regardless of the outcome, I would remain with the party in any capacity. On the other hand if Schreyer was not elected as leader he would not return to provincial politics but would stay in Ottawa. An additional consideration overpowered any question of policy, personality or competence. It was a fact that I had enemies within the party and if elected, a certain number of party members would be disappointed and angry. In contrast, Schreyer was accepted by everyone and my supporters would support him as leader if he were elected. (The "Paulley for Unity" slogan in the previous campaign made sense in regard to this campaign.)

As the convention drew close, media coverage created an impression that the result was too close to call. The press clearly favoured Schreyer's image as a small-'l' Liberal compared to me. This should have been a problem for Schreyer but as it turned out it was not to be. The NDP's new sense of wanting victory, rather than simply wanting to be the conscience of the legislature, an attitude I had largely inspired, worked ultimately to the benefit of Schreyer.

About 700 delegates attended the convention at the Manitoba Convention Centre, but only 500 of them appeared to be accredited. Based on the banners and conversations with people, I realized that Schreyer would carry the day. This was not a particularly discouraging revelation since I felt that the leadership campaign was merely a prelude to the provincial election.

I had reason to believe that the election would produce, if not an NDP victory, at least a position where New Democrats would have more seats than any other party and Liberals and Conservatives would have to coalesce to form a government. This development would lead inevitably to an NDP government – which was, in effect, the reason I had entered politics.

At the convention Schreyer was nominated by Saul Cherniack and Russ Paulley. I was nominated by law partner Leon Mitchell and Joe Borowski. Borowski's announcement of support for me was greeted with dismayed surprise by Schreyer and particularly Orlikow, who could not believe that a Polish steel worker would vote for a Jewish city lawyer.

The nomination speeches were quite civilized but particular comment must be made about Borowski's address. He was an iconoclast and I knew that I should be prepared for anything. Borowski proceeded to describe his candidate's power in the Manitoba Legislature and his unequaled capacity to smash the Tories.

Then, referring to the *Winnipeg Free Press* support for Schreyer, Borowski asked delegates to carefully consider such endorsement. Pointing at Schreyer he said "If this man is favoured by the *Free Press* he should not be favoured by you." Immediate booing was heard from the Schreyer forces. The comments were regarded as a low blow, which they were. However, for years New Democrats had said that if the *Free Press* supports something, we should not be supporting it. Borowski did nothing more than repeat that thought. Was it any worse than Miller's remarks with respect to the young former Liberals who joined the NDP and supported me? Borowski was criticized while Miller emerged unscathed.

Mention has been made of the fact that there appeared to be 700 delegates but only 500 were registered. Apparently many people either believed or wanted to believe that they had been named as delegates, when in fact they had not. Schreyer came to me and explained their predicament. It was finally decided to set up a separate polling booth for those who claimed to be delegates but lacked proper credentials They would be permitted to vote but their votes would not be counted without further verification if they could affect the results. In fact, the non-accredited line was longer than the accredited line.

The final vote was finally announced. Schreyer received 506 votes and Green 178. The numbers included the non-verified delegates since they could not have affected the results. Schreyer had been legitimately and overwhelmingly elected as leader. After the results were announced I took the microphone and made the simple observation, "If not the premier, would you believe a cabinet minister?" Two days later Schreyer filed nomination papers for the provincial election, in the constituency of Rossmere.

The speeches by the two candidates could not have materially affected the results. I made my usual speech condemning the Conservatives on the issues which I intended to highlight in the provincial election campaign. I said the only issue between the two candidates was who was more capable of organizing the party to the stage where it could win a provincial election and become the government of Manitoba.

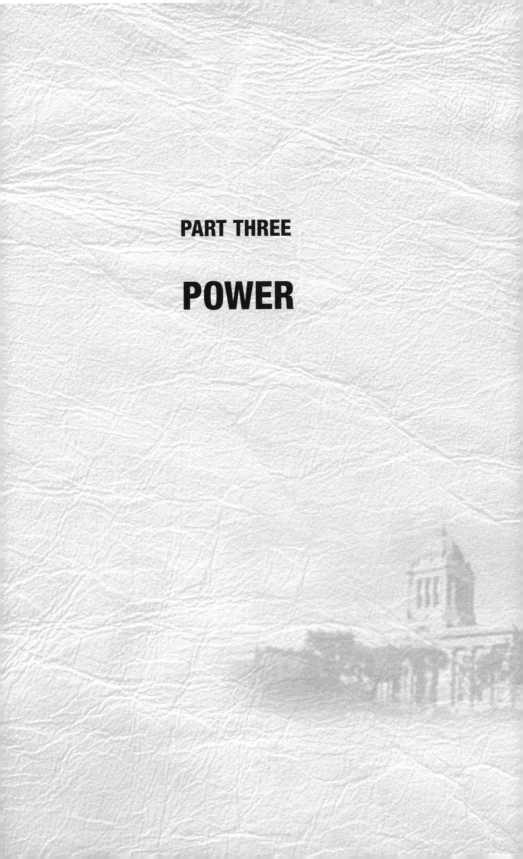

PART THREE

POWER

NDP GOVERNMENT

After Ed Schreyer became leader, the New Democratic Party shifted immediately into the election campaign. The switchover was handled professionally. Party staff had already prepared election literature so that a photograph of either Schreyer or Green could be inserted and could be ready by the following Monday. That night Schreyer, who had resigned his federal seat, was nominated in Rossmere and I was asked by the constituency association to be the guest speaker.

An important feature of the 1969 election campaign, which had significant consequences for the ultimate election and the taking of power by the New Democratic Party, was the Official Languages Act that was being debated in Ottawa.

At a federal/provincial conference, Manitoba Premier Walter Weir took a tough stand against the extension of the French language throughout Canada. This was Pierre Trudeau's number one priority and determined his entry into federal politics. Weir's comments made headlines in Manitoba when he opposed the extension of the French language. He thought it would be to his credit in the election campaign as he followed a pattern which was characteristic of Canadian politics at that time and remains to this day.

Both Schreyer and I recognized the desirability of having a country where ethnic nationalism did not depend on the recognition of one or the other group as dominant. The concept of bilingualism in Canada stemmed from its origins when there was Upper Canada and Lower Canada; Upper Canada was predominantly English and Lower Canada predominantly French. The French language was recognized as a characteristic of our country but the rise of separatism in Quebec provoked a negative reaction, particularly in western Canada where the French constituted a very small percentage of the population in most areas.

I chose the French/English characteristic of Canada as a major topic in my speech at the Schreyer nominating meeting. I stressed that Canada's nationalism was distinct from most other countries. It was not based on a dominant ethnic group. Canada was based on respect for differences between ethnic groups. I maintained that respect went beyond French and English and worked to the advantage of other ethnic groups who had come to this country.

Because I spoke at the nominating meeting for the NDP leader, it was reported in newspapers, on television and on radio. The next day Schreyer received a complaint that I was costing the party votes in north Winnipeg. Rheal Tiffaine, a prominent Conservative of the French-speaking community in St. Boniface, also said my comments would cost the NDP votes. I disagreed, insisting that the French/English dichotomy in Canada was an electoral advantage rather than a disadvantage.

After receiving these complaints, Schreyer tried to convince me to modify and possibly keep silent about the French question for the balance of the election campaign. Fortuitously, while our discussion was taking place, Schreyer received a phone call from his own campaign manager. The individual apparently told him that people in the Rossmere constituency were so impressed with my comments about the French/English issue that they wanted copies of the speech. Schreyer put down the phone, looked at me and said, "You go ahead and make that speech whenever you want to and issue a press release whenever you make it."

The language question did arise during the campaign and Schreyer took the same position that he had always taken. He was very positive towards official bilingualism in this country. This was disconcerting to some New Democrats who were of the unilingual bent.

During the campaign, most New Democrats believed the party would make a good showing but saw no real possibility of forming a government. Nevertheless some of the ambitious ideas involved in my leadership slogan, "Ready To Govern", were contagious and spread to many others in the party. However, since they did not want to use a slogan chosen by the loser, ultimately the NDP election slogan became "Heading For Government."

The vigour of the NDP caucus from 1966 to 1969 and the excitement stimulated by the leadership campaigns of 1968 and 1969 had rejuvenated the party long before Schreyer became leader. Nominations were contested in many constituencies and when nominations closed, the NDP had a full slate of 57 candidates for the first time in its political history. The candidates included distinguished people from all walks of life.

The campaign itself had no special interest and created little enthusiasm, but one of the more comical features was a speech by former leader Russ Paulley. Reports indicated that he had said the people of Manitoba should follow Ed Schreyer who would then lead them down the garden path. While Paulley may have been well fortified when he made those remarks, considering his past rhetoric, it is possible that he believed Manitobans would regard this statement as a positive one.

Bobby Bend, the new Liberal leader, seized on the statement and tried to make an issue of it. To regard a statement by a former leader, who was now virtually a nonentity in the party, as something to treat seriously was indicative of Bend's lack of political acumen.

Bend became the Liberal party leader shortly before the election. Veteran Liberal parliamentarian D.L.Campbell had given up his seat in Lakeside so the leader would be able to sit in the Legislature. Bend was not elected and Conservative Harry Enns who, because of redistribution of electoral boundaries was also running in Lakeside, won. Campbell, who may well have been re-elected, probably facilitated in making Enns the longest-serving member in the legislature until his recent retirement. He sat continuously from 1966 to 2003.

On election night, just before the results started to come in, MP David Orlikow came to the committee rooms shared by Cherniack, Hanuschak and myself. He told me that he was certain the NDP would become the official opposition. The prediction astonished me. On the night of the leadership campaign after Schreyer aand I had spoken, Orlikow said on the air that with me as the leader the New Democratic Party would become the opposition, but with Schreyer the party would become the government. I had believed Orlikow was sincere about what he was saying. Apparently that was not the case.

If Schreyer could merely lead the party to second place, what was all the excitement about? Being the official Opposition would not be a success. I indicated to Orlikow that the party would win more seats than any other party. I didn't go any further because I couldn't predict the party would win enough seats to form the government. (In the 57-seat Manitoba legislature, a party must win 29 seats in order to have a majority.) Schreyer's prediction was much more accurate. Just before election day he told me that he could count up to twenty-seven seats but couldn't find the additional two to form a government.

When the results came in the night of June 25th, the New Democrats had won 28 seats, one short of the magic number. The ultimate outcome was unpredictable. (I won the Inkster riding with 71 per cent of the vote, the highest percentage by any candidate running in a three-way race).

At the victory celebration at the Union Centre there was mass euphoria. The party faithful saw the opportunity for the "New Jerusalem" which they had sought for so many years. The farthest thing from anyone's mind were practical considerations involved in running a government. The New Democrats believed they were going to bring about social justice and saw no reason why this would not be possible and feasible.

When I got home that night I examined the results and immediately called Schreyer. I told him that I knew who might be the twenty-ninth member. The man was Larry Desjardins, the Liberal member for St. Boniface. I did not believe Desjardins could be part of a government led by Walter Weir, because of the reasons he was in politics. Desjardins' priorities were public aid to Roman Catholic schools and official status for the French language in Manitoba and Canada. On both of these issues Weir would not be the answer. Immediately grasping the importance of these issues, Schreyer soon met with Desjardins.

Meanwhile rumours circulated about the free enterprise parties attempting to prevent a takeover by the New Democrats, whom they regarded as communists. In particular, they were concerned about me being a member of the government. Therefore discussions were being held about forming a government which would combine Liberals, Conservatives and Jake Froese, the lone Social Credit member. The concept called for Weir to step aside and Gildas Molgat, the respected former Liberal leader, to form a government. In the view of those who supported this concept, the result would be an ideologically sound government with little controversy.

But the originators of this plan did not reckon with Desjardins. He could not become a member of such a coalition. Furthermore he had an affinity with Schreyer's liberalism and was pleased with the leader's apparent support for Desjardins' stance on language questions. However he did not share my economic views. Desjardins calculated that with Schreyer as leader, the government would be moderate. He was probably given reason to believe that Schreyer would achieve his longstanding objective of providing some aid for Roman Catholic schools.

Therefore Desjardins indicated his willingness to sit on the government side. He could not and would not become a New Democrat because of his long condemnation of the party's economic policies but he did believe he could support it and would sit with the caucus as a Liberal Democrat.

I tried to convince Desjardins that the Liberal Democrat designation would create a problem. I was willing to forego Desjardins' participation altogether if he did not become a New Democrat. Schreyer was far more practical and decided the MLA's position could be accepted if he committed to support the government – which he did.

With that commitment, Weir's government resigned and the Lieutenant Governor called on Ed Schreyer to form a government in the Province of Manitoba. On July 25, 1969 Manitoba had its first NDP government.

There is a feature of the 1969 election campaign that deserves further comment.

The number one issue put forward by the NDP was the unfairness of the system of paying for medicare. The Conservative government insisted on premiums which would tax all families equally, regardless of income. Walter Weir argued that, if there was to be medical care insurance, he wanted the people of the province to know that it wasn't free.

During the 1968 legislative session, the NDP caucus vigorously attacked this form of financing medicare. They agreed that the public should know how the program was being paid for but insisted that taxes rather than premiums was a fairer system since they would be based on the ability of the citizen to pay. The government prevailed and the premium system was put ito effect.

The election was scheduled to take place on June 25, 1969. The first premium notice had, as a matter of routine, been scheduled to be sent out during the last two weeks of June. This was totally overlooked by the Conservative administration and it is quite likely that none of the senior civil personnel alerted the government to the schedule. As a result a vital piece of election propaganda was sent out to every family in Manitoba about two weeks before the election. It was the invoices for medical care premiums. It alerted the citizens to the most important issue of the NDP campaign in a way which couldn't be duplicated by any amount of election engineering, speech-making, handing out of pamphlets or other form of propaganda. I suspect that the scheduling of the medicare premium notice was not simply an accident or the normal chain of events.

A government and an administration do not always see eye to eye. In this case the administrative officers concerned were engaged in working to rule, that is, they were doing exactly what the schedule required them to do. No one took the trouble of alerting the politicians to what would ultimately be a devastating blow to the political fortunes of the Progressive Conservative party.

The medical premium statements probably had more to do with the election of the NDP government than the leadership change, the slickness of our campaign or any other feature of the NDP program. It is an event of which little note has been taken from the time that it occurred to the writing of this book.

When it became apparent that the NDP would form the government, Ed Schreyer faced the challenge of selecting his cabinet. Schreyer believed appointing me as health minister would be viewed as a reward since the first important business would be reduction of medical care premiums.

I would have preferred a more economically oriented portfolio. However I was in no position to argue and prepared to assume my new responsibilities.

Two other appointments deserve mention. Joe Borowski had been criticized for the manner in which he had nominated me at the leadership convention. Several Schreyer supporters viewed him with animosity while the media generally regarded him as a loose cannon. However when Schreyer asked me whether I saw any potential danger in appointing Borowski, I said that Borowski would be an asset to the government.

Ultimately Borowski was appointed minister of highways and became one of the most popular ministers until his falling out with the party on the issue of abortion several years later. He left the NDP and ultimately ran as an independent in 1973, when he was defeated by Rev. Donald Malinowski,. This should have been a warning for others who left the party and challenged the NDP in future elections. They included myself and subsequently Russell Doern.

Ben Hanuschak was a supporter of mine. Between 1966 and 1969 he had been a prominent and effective MLA as well as being involved in the party organization as provincial secretary. Hanuschak had been the only MLA who did not sign the 1969 declaration which disowned Russ Paulley and endorsed Schreyer as the future leader. But because of his decision, Hanuschak was viewed by colleagues as a Green supporter and a traitor to their cause. He continued to support me in the 1969 leadership race.

In 1966, Hanuschak had won the Burrows seat against a prominent Liberal candidate and was re-elected with a substantial majority in 1969. One of the most distinguished New Democrat MLAs in terms of community achievement, he was fully bilingual in Ukrainian and English and had degrees in law and education. He seemed to be an obvious choice for a cabinet post but when the cabinet was announced, his name was not included.

I was distressed by that omission and spoke to Schreyer, who told me that colleagues had told him Hanuschak had been involved in some legal improprieties in the Interlake when he was an articling clerk. The allegations were vague and I knew nothing about them. I asked Hanuschak and was told that there was no validity to the allegation. I then resumed talks with Schreyer about the manner in which the MLA was being treated. Schreyer appointed Hanuschak to be the speaker of the House and ultimately took him into the cabinet as Minister of Education.

The first years of the NDP government saw a true revolution in Manitoba politics. Not only were there radical changes in legislation and the manner in which the government performed, there were also changes in the operation of the House and public reaction to such measures.

Except on rare occasions, before 1969 and after 1979, relatively few people sat in the public gallery to watch the MLAs in action. Although there were some regulars and some school children who were brought by teachers for a brief view of the legislative process, for the most part the seats were empty. This changed dramatically in 1970 during debate on public automobile insurance. Night after night the gallery was crowded with observers and seating space was at a premium. Later when the legislation went to committee, even more people crowded the committee room to make presentations or just to watch the historic event. Never before had such scenes been witnessed. It was a true indication of public involvement during the first four years of the Schreyer administration as the government hammered out its mandated program.

Another change occurred with much less fanfare. For many years the Speaker had opened each sitting of the Legislature with a prayer as all members stood in observance. Few actually paid much attention. But what was being said was an endorsement of the divine right of kings. The actual words were: "Oh eternal and almighty God by whom kings rule and make equitable laws, give us the wisdom to make such laws . . ."

Listening to a doctrine which expounded the divine right of kings – something that had been thoroughly discredited in all of the history books – always made me uncomfortable. Hanuschak and I looked at the prayer and came to the conclusion that changes were required. The question was how to make the change. Any debate in the Legislature concerning the prayer would be highly divisive and would raise the hackles of traditionalists on an issue which was really of no importance.

We looked for the origin of this prayer. When we found no mandate in the rules or any other parliamentary authorities for that particular prayer, we decided on a peremptory plan. No resolution would be introduced. Instead Hanuschak would simply recite a slightly different prayer and bring about a *fait accompli*. The prayer would be almost identical to the one previously recited, but the phrase "by whom kings rule and make equitable laws" would be omitted.

On the first day of the first legislative session, Hanuschak took off the Speaker's hat, looked inside its crown where the typed prayer was placed for the Speaker's assistance and read, "Oh eternal and almighty God, give us the wisdom to make such laws . . ." Some members of the Legislature noticed the omission and others did not, but the prayer was changed without one word of debate or criticism.

In the late 1970s there was one attempt to change the legislative prayer when Rev. Malinowski proposed that the daily proceeding begin with the Lord's prayer. I was offended by an attempt to insert a denominational prayer into the legislative proceedings. I indicated that while I did not want to initiate a divisive debate, Malinowski's proposal could precipitate such action. I proposed an alternative – several moments of silence at the beginning of each sitting where each member could contemplate whatever he wished in regard to divine inspiration. Malinowski was convinced not to proceed with his proposal. To date, the prayer, as it was first read in August 1969, is still read on a daily basis.

Green mesmerizes the NDP front bench, Ed Schreyer, near right and Howard Pawley, far right.

Green shares a laugh with former Liberal Premier Douglas Campbell.

POWER

I never made any pretence about my objectives in seeking political office. I wanted power. I made no protestation, as other politicians sometimes do, that I was not power-hungry. I believed that any politician who said otherwise was fooling himself, trying to fool everyone else, or both.

In order to obtain power I had left a profitable and promising law practice for the life of a politician with its vagaries, uncertainties and lesser income. My main motivation was a belief that one could use power to make things better. Another strong motivation for wanting power was to keep others from having power over me. In my view, the only way to avoid being controlled was to control the power.

In 1969 the New Democratic Party achieved a measure of power. Because the party did so on the basis of certain well-defined objectives, there was little confusion in my mind as to what the government was going to do. The major planks in the election platform were:

1. Elimination of medicare premiums to be substituted by some other form of taxation, preferably income tax.
2. Creation of a public automobile insurance corporation to underwrite all automobile insurance in the province.
3. Unification of Greater Winnipeg.
4. A review of the hydro development program which would have displaced an Indian community at South Indian Lake.

There were other issues but these were peculiarly identified with me from the time I entered politics until power was achieved.

However it quickly became apparent to me and my colleagues that the issues and commitments which appeared to have been so well defined prior to the election would not be implemented without a battle. This battle was not mainly with the Opposition. It was rooted in the NDP caucus itself.

The most prominent election issue was the elimination of medicare premiums. When the caucus first met, that subject was raised immediately. Surprisingly there was no unanimity about whether it was a good idea. Saul Miller, a close confidant of Schreyer, was adamantly opposed to the elimination of the premiums because it would reduce the ability of the province to give relief to municipal taxation – one of his most important priorities.

Intense debate took place on what one should have been the most non-debatable item but Schreyer quickly realized that with a substantial majority of caucus members so intent on eliminating medicare premiums, there was no turning back. The caucus decided this issue would be the number one priority of the session to be held in fall.

The strategy of the session was simple: pass the spending estimates that had been tabled by the Conservative government before the election and convert the medicare premiums into a different form of taxation. This strategy placed the Conservatives in a quandary. They could not very well oppose their own spending estimates with any degree of credibility.

The legislature was called in August 14, 1969 and the throne speech indicated the direction of the government. The spending estimates were introduced and, as Health Minister, I announced that the premiums relating to medicare would be reduced by 88 per cent.

Schreyer believed that totally eliminating the premiums would in some way affect the manner in which they would be collected if they were ever re-imposed in the future. This did not appear to be a real fear since there was no intention of imposing the premiums again. Nevertheless the announcement of premium elimination went ahead and for all practical purposes, the public accepted the fact that the New Democrats had acted on their major election promise.

On the same day that I announced the elimination of medicare premiums, Finance Minister Saul Cherniack announced that corporate and personal income taxes would be increased to make up for the revenue shortfall caused by the premium reduction.

From that day critics, most notably the Conservatives, repeatedly charged that Manitoba had the highest income tax rates in Canada. Apparently the Conservatives were of the view that a middle-class taxpayer was better off paying $300 a year for medicare premiums instead of $100 a year in additional income tax. The argument, which continued for years only had validity to those who did not consider the payment of premiums as a form of taxation.

Those who accepted that premiums were also a tax, realized Manitoba taxpayers paid less than their counterparts in other provinces.

The virtual elimination of medicare premiums was to come into effect on January 1, 1970. In December 1969 a pivotal event took place. Cherniack came into a meeting of cabinet immediately after a telephone conference with representatives of a leading financial institution in the province.

Cherniack said the discussion had not been based on politics but rather on pure pragmatism. The spokesmen for the institution had merely noted that if the corporate income tax did increase, the institution would be looking to move its head office to one of the Maritime provinces where the corporate tax would be reduced.

Again Cherniack insisted this was not a political move but rather a financially pragmatic move. That statement was greeted with several seconds of silence. I broke the silence. I said, "There are two board rooms where meetings are taking place at the present time. One board room is at the financial institution. The other board room is the cabinet room. The question that we have to decide is not whether or not the medical premiums will be reduced and the income tax increased. The real question is: "In which room does the Government of Manitoba sit?"

The question was answered quickly. Schreyer advised Cherniack to inform the financial institution that the government intended to proceed with its plan. That ended the threat to the medicare premium plan. Whether or not the financial institution moved their head office was of no consequence. As a result the Schreyer administration continued to function as a viable institution during all its years in office.

The unification of Winnipeg and the introduction of public automobile insurance involved more controversy than did the medicare premiums where the controversy was more internal. These subjects are discussed later.

The New Democratic Party government assumed its responsibilities as government with the same difficulties and problems normally associated with any change of government. Administrative measures, which constitute at least 95 per cent of governmental authority, were handled by a competent and effective cabinet. If anything, Schreyer's cabinet was composed of people who were generally more qualified academically than those in the previous government and had many years of public administration experience.

I was the Minister of Health between July 1969 and December 1969. I then became the Minister of Mines and Natural Resources, which was more in keeping with my economic objectives, and took over the role of House leader because of my recognized skill in dealing with legislative matters.

When I was first elected to the Legislature, I admitted that I was illiterate insofar as the Canadian languages were concerned. I spoke English, but not French. I indicated my intention to become literate in the second language and for the next three years took French lessons from a private tutor, Madame Madelaine Morissutti. By the time the NDP came to power I could speak a workable French. Those language skills were improved when I attended a federally-sponsored immersion course for civil servants in Quebec City. (I was in Quebec City during the October 1970 crises but walked the streets without difficulty.)

My fluency in French was a definite asset and enabled me to travel extensively. Whenever there was a French-oriented international conference, the federal government would send a delegation composed of a federal minister and four provincial ministers representing Quebec, Ontario, New Brunswick and Manitoba, all of which were recognized as having a significant French presence.

Naturally the representatives should speak the language. The Manitoba cabinet contained only two ministers who spoke French, myself and Rene Toupin. Since the Premier rarely designated himself as a delegate the odds were very good that I would be sent. As a result I attended federal/provincial conferences in Togo, the Central African Republic, the Ivory Coast, France, Madagascar and Argentina.

The 1976 trip to Argentina caused a bit of controversy in the legislature. I attended as the vice-chairman of the provincial delegation to a United Nations conference. On my return I sported a wonderful tan as a result of some time spent on the beaches.

Opposition Leader Sidney Spivak, now deceased, got up in the House and made a derogatory reference to a minister sunning himself at public expense on a junket. Unrepentant, I responded by saying I enjoyed the wonderful ministerial perks which enabled me to travel extensively in Canada and overseas. Not only did I fulfill my duties as the province's representative on these trips, I also enjoyed myself. In contrast, I could recall that when Spivak was a cabinet minister and was required to make numerous trips to other countries and other provinces, he was always miserable. I added that my purpose in life was to keep Spivak out of his misery.

There can be no doubt that the first term of the Schreyer government was successful. Misgivings about the elimination of medicare premiums vanished. Unicity was created and exists to this day. The Manitoba Public Insurance Company was created and has proved of great benefit to Manitobans. In the 1973 budget the hospital premiums were also eliminated, making Manitoba a leader in provincial taxation by eliminating all hospital and medical premiums and financing these programs out of general taxation.

Power has its fringe benefits. It gives one the capacity to undo injustice. Governor Dukakis of Massachusetts used power to pardon Sacco and Vancetti who were executed in the late 1920s, after being unjustly convicted of murder. The proceedings against them were tantamount to a juridical assassination. Although Dukakis could not undo their execution he did give a posthumous pardon.

My own use of power to undo injustice involved the late Solomon Greenberg, a lawyer who practised in Manitoba. Mr. Greenberg was one of the most outstanding lawyers in Winnipeg but was never recognized by the powers-that-be with the honour of becoming a Q.C. This was because Mr. Greenberg was considered a leftist who had acted on behalf of communists when they were under attack. By the time the NDP came to power Mr. Greenberg had passed away. At the very first opportunity, in December 1969, I initiated a move in cabinet to confer a posthumous Q.C. on Solomon Greenberg. To my knowledge this is the only such recognition ever conferred in the British Commonwealth.

As far as I was concerned, the government's action from 1969 to 1973 was a fulfillment of my commitments when I entered politics. I was able to campaign in the 1973 election by detailing promises I had made during my time in Opposition and showing how each of the promises had been kept.

A SECOND TERM

In its first term the New Democratic Party government accomplished all the major program objectives included in its 1969 election platform. By 1973, after glossing over differences with respect to public aid to private schools, (and my return to Cabinet following resignation on that issue) the priority of the government and the party was to prepare for the next election.

Since the government had fulfilled most of promises made in the previous campaign, it had laid a very successful foundation for this contest. Indeed when an election pamphlet was discussed by the election committee, I produced the 1969 pamphlet and showed the NDP had fulfilled the majority of those commitments. Since virtually all of them had been fulfilled, I suggested the 1973 pamphlet be an exact reproduction of the earlier one, with check marks showing the New Democratic Party had kept its promises. The theme of the election would be "Keep Your Government Yours."

Meanwhile, Ed Schreyer had assumed responsibility as Minister of Finance, after Saul Cherniack left the portfolio, and prepared to introduce the budget for the 1973 session. The government's fiscal record was very positive. Virtually balanced budgets had been presented every year and none of the major initiatives accomplished during the four years involved additional spending. As well, because the general economy in Canada was positive, the inflationary cycle created a favourable financial balance for the government.

The situation inspired Schreyer to produce a budget which offered almost $63 million in tax relief. Although the Premier had only moderately supported the elimination of medicare premiums in 1969, he now threw caution to the wind and eliminated the remainder of the premiums, as well as all of the hospital premiums.

This action devastated the Opposition. At that time Sidney Spivak was the Conservative leader, while the new Liberal leader was tax lawyer Izzy Asper.

The budget stunned them and their parties into virtual silence. Unable to attack the document they attempted to delay the closing of the legislature in the forlorn hope that by the fall, the positive atmosphere created by Schreyer would have waned. Those extensive attempts to prolong the session were unsuccessful. On May 25, 1973 the legislature was dissolved and Schreyer announced an election would be held on June 28, 1973.

Generally the election campaign went well for the NDP. One of the less palatable features was the tendency of some to focus on the fact that both Spivak and Asper were River Heights Jewish lawyers. On one occasion Schreyer referred to them as 'shyster' lawyers and, at other times, as the River Heights "gold dust twins." Finally Cherniack pleaded with Schreyer to desist from adding fuel to this fire.

The campaign ended in an NDP victory but without the expected margin – we received 42.1 per cent of the vote, up from 38.1 per cent in the previous election. Many supporters regarded this as less than overwhelming victory and attributed it to two incidents.

While speaking in the Roblin area, Schreyer stated that, while Wally McKenzie, the member for that riding, had received favourable treatment from the government, he, Schreyer, was no longer interested nor did he intend to deal fairly with "malicious MLAs." That speech was reported on the newspapers' front pages during the weekend before the vote and many believed it had an unfavorable impact and reduced the New Democrat Party's margin of victory.

As well, during a television debate with Izzy Asper, I was angered by some of Asper's outrageous statements. Responding in what I acknowledge to be my least satisfactory, angry manner, I displayed a side of myself that would have been better restrained.

Nevertheless the New Democrats won the election and almost all cabinet members were returned. An exception was Al Mackling who went down to defeat in St. James. He and other anti-Green party members blamed the defeat on the legislation which unified greater Winnipeg.

In actuality, the defeat was more likely due to Mackling's attitude of moral superiority and his unilateral decision to commence criminal prosecutions against a movie house which was showing "The Last Tango in Paris." The decision was made without any cabinet consultation and many ministers reacted angrily when presented with the *fait accompli*. Mackling however, could not morally condone the showing of a movie which contained explicit, albeit simulated sex. Therefore, completely on his own, he took steps to prosecute the theatre. Possibly many people in St. James felt that Mackling had no right to tell them what movies they could or could not watch.

In all other suburbs NDP members were re-elected and in many other areas the majorities were increased.

The second term of the New Democratic Party government proved to be less dramatic than the first one. It preferred to consolidate and govern in a more conservative manner than in the past. Furthermore no new major initiatives were planned for this term. That does not mean no new steps were taken, but none could compare with the dramatic changes undertaken from 1969 to 1973.

I was involved in several initiatives. The most important concerned mineral royalty taxes. A new policy change, which was achieved through regulation, required every new mining exploration program to have the public as its partner to the tune of 50 per cent.

The public, however, was not given a free ride. The government was required to participate dollar for dollar in any exploration program and, if proved successful, the government would be a partner in the development to the extent of fifty percent. This program went into effect after consultation with the mining companies involved. By and large it was accepted.

While the mining companies resented any attempt by government to take over any of their existing activities, they did not show the same resistance to accepting the government as a paying partner, just as they would accept any other paying partner.

However the Opposition and the media attacked the government and predicted that mining exploration in the province would dry up. I responded by saying the same level of exploration that had taken place in the past would continue in the future. And if there was any slacking off in the private sector, the public sector would take up the slack.

In actual fact the mining exploration program in the province proceeded undiminished and the government was a fifty-per-cent partner in all new exploration programs.

The anti-government media also accused me of gambling with public money because this program would result in the drilling of dry wells and unsuccessful exploration for new mines. This was a valid attack. Many millions of dollars are spent on exploration in order to find one mine. It was entirely possible that the government's investment would wind up with no return, just as private sector money often does.

Fortuitously one government exploration program involving a Swedish company, Granges Explorations, did result in the discovery of a mine. The public participated in the ownership of this mine for the remaining years of the NDP administration and several years thereafter. Not until the early 1990s was the public share of this mine sold to the private sector by the Filmon government who was embarrassed by public success. As a result of the sale, virtually every cent of the investment by the people of Manitoba during the NDP mining program was recovered.

The other initiative in the mining field was a mining tax based on the recovery of economic rent. The government had commissioned Eric Kierans, a former federal Liberal cabinet minister and a prominent economist, to conduct a review of mining taxation in Manitoba.

Kierans produced a report which was far more radical than anything envisaged by the New Democratic Party. In effect, he suggested that taxation should result in mining companies ultimately turning over their existing works to the government. I said I would not tax the mining companies out of existence. If I wanted to obtain ownership, I would expropriate them with appropriate compensation. But I had no intention of doing so. Mining companies that had invested in Manitoba were entitled to a reasonable return on their investment. The province would have the same advantages.

My philosophy called for the public to have the same commitment to investment as the mining companies. In this regard, I did agree with a fundamental proposition advanced by Kierans: the public should be entitled to a fair share of the economic rent which resulted when the value of the mining resources exceeded legitimate expectations.

Extensive meetings were held with the departments of finance and mines and a tax was eventually developed which guaranteed a mining company would receive a reasonable return for its investment. When that return exceeded reasonable expectations because of increases in price, the province would share the benefits.

The new tax was vigorously opposed by the Opposition and the mining companies but ultimately was passed by the Legislature in June 1974.

There is a sequel to the mining tax story. When the Conservative government assumed power in 1977, it repealed the mining tax legislation. When Howard Pawley's NDP government was elected in 1981 it did not reimpose this tax, primarily because it did not want to suggest anything done by the Schreyer administration was worthy of reinstatement.

During the second session of the legislature I was given the task of stabilizing the activities of the Manitoba Development Corporation. Those activities were stabilized but not until the government had been compelled to sustain considerable losses by some of the previous recipients of government loans.

The new philosophy with regard to the fund is exemplified by the loan to McCain Foods, a huge national enterprise engaged in the food business. The Manitoba Development Corporation made a viable commercial loan to the company, which became a major industry in rural Manitoba.

Another feature of the government's second term was the advancement of the concept of treasury branches. Always part of New Democratic Party policy, it called for the province to establish its own bank.

This was not purely socialist doctrine. As a matter of fact, the only treasury branches existing in Canada had been established by the Social Credit government of Alberta. They were very successful and gave the government a foot in the door of the financial institutions of the province.

The concept of treasury branches was vigorously advanced by some members of the Manitoba cabinet and as vigorously rejected by others. In particular Saul Miller, who had become the Minister of Finance, was very reluctant to introduce such legislation because he believed it would label the New Democratic Party as a radically socialist government, a label which he eschewed.

Despite that resistance, the government ultimately brought in legislation calling for the establishment of treasury branches. Because I was actively involved in the debate of this subject, members of the Opposition said the bill was being introduced because the minister of mines wanted to own a bank. I responded by saying there was nothing unusual about wanting to own a bank and if wants alone were the issue, I would want to own all the banks.

However, I said, the government was engaged in a modest proposal to establish its own treasury branch, similar to what had occurred in non-socialist Alberta. The legislation was passed but Miller took no steps to implement the program. The legislation remained on the books for many years but no treasurey banks were erected.

Another initiative worthy of mention was taken by Agriculture Minister Sam Uskiw. He wanted to provide a land option to farmers. There was a saying that the farmers in Manitoba lived poor and died rich. This was because so much of their money was invested in land and so little return was received from their operations. When farmers died, their land usually had increased substantially in value, but they had not benefited from their investments during their lifetime.

Uskiw introduced a program which enabled land-owning farmers to be relieved of their financial burden by allowing them to operate lands at a fair rent and the results of their labours during their lifetime. The program was not mandatory and simply provided an option to the rural community. It was attacked vigorously by rural Conservative MLAs as a move towards communism. The publicly-owned land system ultimately became part of the NDP program and was implemented. It did not survive the defeat in 1977 and was not a feature of the Pawley administration in the 1980s.

Towards the end of the government's second term an important incident took place in cabinet. Schreyer called a cabinet meeting and indicated his intention to resign. Apparently he had been offered a post by the Trudeau administration and appeared ready to accept it.

Rather than lead the New Democrats into an election for a third term, he either saw the writing on the wall or was using his resignation as a cloak to deal with the cabinet and the party for rejecting his initiative to provide public aid to private schools.

His departure would place the party in an impossible position because many believed the only reason the NDP was in power was because of Schreyer.

Cabinet was stunned by the announcement. I was the first to respond. I told the Premier that the party had made a great investment in him. Furthermore I said Schreyer had contributed to the atmosphere which would put the party in an impossible position. If the Premier resigned, I said I would also resign. Then it could be argued that the party's disarray was not due to Schreyer's resignation but rather to various resignations.

There followed a hasty consultation between Schreyer and his principle colleagues, Cherniack and Miller. After a short time, the Premier withdrew his resignation and the party prepared for the coming election.

That race was complicated by two major developments – wage and price controls and the Griffin Steel strike. Both were related to the NDP's relationship with trade unions and affected my status as a member of the New Democratic Party.

During the 1970s dramatic increases in wages and prices resulted in double-digit inflation. The Trudeau government was re-elected on the specific promise not to impose wage and price controls which had been advocated by Conservative leader Robert Stanfield.

After the election, however, the Trudeau government saw no alternative but to impose the same controls which it had opposed. Late in 1975, all premiers attended a conference in Ottawa. Schreyer then returned to Manitoba and told his cabinet he had agreed that Manitoba would endorse a system of wage and price controls because they could only be implemented nationwide if every province agreed to cooperate.

The Premier made this decision unilaterally without any cabinet or caucus consultation. I had always opposed any interference with free collective bargaining and viewed wage and price controls as a profound interference. Indicating my dissatisfaction to Schreyer, I asked whether the province would be required to enact legislation to implement controls. In that case, I would have difficulty supporting such a bill.

After the issue was examined it was determined that the province could participate in the national measure through an order-in-council by cabinet. This circumvented a vote where my opposition would be recorded, but it also made me subject to cabinet solidarity and a *de facto* supporter of wage and price control.

The major complication of the Manitoba government entering into this arrangement was the opposition to such controls expressed by the national New Democratic Party and the trade union movement. The trade unions were particularly vigorous and venomous. Various forms of protest were held and the Manitoba government was roundly criticized for entering the program.

The matter came to a head at the NDP convention which was called for January 1975. This was to be the last such gathering before a provincial election and the party bureaucracy, as well as the trade union movement, were determined to rebuke the government for having entered into the wage and price control measure.

Schreyer was a prime target as resolutions were prepared which created the anomaly of New Democratic Party members condemning the New Democratic Party government. The trade unions aligned themselves with the militant feminists in an arrangement where those who had previously been cold to one another now found peculiar support. They apparently operated on the principle that the enemy of my enemy is my friend and the Schreyer government was the enemy of both groups.

The feminists had made some progress in receiving support from various elements of the government but the majority of the cabinet was not sympathetic to their more extreme proposals.

At the convention, NDP president Muriel Smith presided and attempted to begin the proceedings with a song opposed to wage and price control. I immediately took the floor on a point of order and challenged the item because it was not part of the agenda and would prejudice debate on an important issue.

My challenge was upheld and the song, the words of which had been distributed to all delegates, was put aside. Debate on wage and price control dominated the proceedings. Much to the chagrin of the trade union people and federal NDP representatives, particularly MP David Orlikow, I led the defence of the government's action. I argued that while I was opposed to controls generally and was an acknowledged fighter for the free collective bargaining process, this resolution would have no practical result except public condemnation of the government.

Because the government had legally bound itself to co-operate with the controls, it could not honourably extricate itself from this commitment. Therefore the prospect of NDP members condemning a NDP government would have no practical result and did not make sense.

Ultimately, despite successive attempts at compromise by Len Stevens, head of the Manitoba Federation of Labour, the resolution declaring opposition to controls was defeated.

During this convention I laid the foundation for my ultimate downfall. In the past the trade union movement had been my strongest supporter because of my history of defending the free collective bargaining process and acting as a lawyer on behalf of most major unions. Now those unions were expressing dismay because I did not support their stand against Schreyer in regard to wage and price controls.

On the other hand the feminists had always regarded me as an enemy since I had not readily accepted some of their more militant positions. In particular I was not a fan of affirmative action, which I viewed as racial discrimination. While I readily approved and accepted the concept of equal pay for equal work, the concept of equal pay for work of equal value made no sense to me.

After the convention the government and the party sought to consolidate and prepare for the election which was likely to be called for the spring or fall of 1977.

The party's campaign message in that election was subject to internal discussion and debate. I reminded members that in 1973 they had been re-elected on a record of achievement and fulfillment of political promises. They also had the advantage of the budget which had given Manitobans $63 million in tax relief. The same approach could not be taken in regard to the second term. Although the government had managed its affairs with relative fiscal responsibility and produced a more or less balanced budget for three of the four years, these achievements could not be compared to the major tax relief of 1973. Such action was impossible in 1977.

As well, the Manitoba Development Corporation, whose losses were becoming apparent, was under constant attack. The size of the losses were now public, a direct result of government policy which required the

Corporation to make reports to the legislature about all investments undertaken by the province.

I took the offensive and began making speeches throughout the province, constantly stressing the theme: "The public can do it." I showed how the problems associated with the Manitoba Development Corporation had, in large part, been caused by commitments made during the Conservative years. I also attempted to show that other provinces and the federal government were engaged in public involvement in commercial development but on a much less businesslike basis. While, for the most part, the Manitoba government had invested in business on the same commercial basis as a bank, other provinces had provided other types of incentives.

I maintained people should have confidence in their own ability to handle their affairs and hoped the theme "The Public Can Do It" would be adopted as the slogan for the coming election. Party bureaucracy, however feared any ideological slogan which might cause controversy. Although they were unhappy with Schreyer's leadership, particularly in regard to wage and price controls, they believed that he was the party's major asset in terms of getting re-elected. They also believed, with some validity, that Schreyer's days were numbered and that if the NDP won he would soon leave the scene.

Herb Schultz, Schreyer's executive assistant, and a long time Green supporter also believed the re-election of the New Democratic Party depended on Schreyer. As far as he was concerned, Sterling Lyon, who had taken over the Conservative leadership from Sidney Spivak, was not regarded by the public as a trustworthy person.

Therefore he coined the slogan "Leadership you can trust", hoping the public would look at both leaders and choose Schreyer. I adamantly opposed this slogan. I did not believe that Schreyer was any more honest and trustworthy than Lyon. Nor did I accept the conventional party mythology that the NDP was morally superior to the Liberals or the Conservatives.

Arguing that the difference was based on ideas rather than morality, I did not perceive my NDP colleagues as more morally pure than those of the other parties. I had many friends of Liberal and Conservative persuasion and respected them. I was adamantly opposed to Conservative policies and ideology, but I did not oppose individual Conservatives on the basis of their integrity.

Despite my argument, the bureaucracy and Schultz won and the New Democratic Party went to the public with the slogan "Leadership you can trust."

Unlike the previous two contests the 1977 campaign lacked the same level of conflict about issues. When it was over the New Democratic Party was defeated. Although Schreyer noted the shift of 400 votes in various ridings would have resulted in the re-election of the New Democratic Party, the party had lost.

The composition of the Manitoba legislature assembly had changed. The Conservatives had 33 seats, New Democratic Party 23, and the Liberals one. The New Democratic Party was back on the opposition benches but with 23 seats had a much stronger base than when it was last in opposition. In 1966 the party had only 11 seats. The NDP received 38 per cent of the vote which was almost equal to the percentage which had put the party in power in 1969.

PART FOUR

THE BIG ISSUES

PUBLIC AUTOMOBILE INSURANCE

Without doubt the most fundamental reform contained in the 1969 election platform was the public automobile insurance program.

In the 1950s public automobile insurance was instituted by Tommy Douglas's CCF government in Saskatchewan. Subsequent independent surveys showed it to be a most effective and efficient automobile insurance program.

In Manitoba, public auto insurance had been an important feature of the CCF and then the NDP platforms. From 1966 to 1969 it was almost automatic for the party to introduce an amendment to the Throne speech resolution, calling upon the government to institute a public automobile insurance scheme. Equally automatic was the opposition to such a move by both the Liberals and Conservatives who would vote together to defeat the amendment.

When the NDP became government it was time to act. The first session was supposed to be brief but actually lasted several months as the new ministers were persuaded to bring in new legislation and programs.

After prorogation, the NDP caucus met to consider the strategy for the next session. The majority assumed that a public insurance plan would be a top priority. However almost immediately after the election, the Premier was receiving representations from the insurance industry, lobbying against such a program.

Such action appeared to have some impact because Schreyer finally announced the formation of a committee to deal with the matter, with Howard Pawley as the minister in charge. At a subsequent cabinet meeting it was decided to make it clear that this committee was not going to review the question of whether this policy should be instituted. Instead its purpose was to examine the method of implementation. It would be headed by R.D. Blackburn, a previous chief executive officer of the Saskatchewan plan.

Shortly thereafter Pawley was invited to a dinner meeting with representatives of the automobile insurance industry. Following the meeting he informed me that the insurance people said they wanted the meeting because they didn't know where they stood with him. They told him that if I had been appointed they would have known where they stood.

When the caucus met to consider the coming session, two surprising and disconcerting developments occurred. Several ministers questioned whether the government should proceed with so momentous a program. I was adamant the program be proceeded with. I argued that if this relatively simple economic initiative, which had no financial cost associated with its implementation, did not proceed, it was tantamount to confessing an inability to achieve any of the social and economic changes which the party had advocated for so many years.

This argument did not convince Larry Desjardins and his attitude was a harbinger of things to come. A long-time anti-socialist member of the legislature, Desjardins vigorously opposed what he viewed as the radical socialism of the NDP. Now he was in a caucus which was considering the public underwriting of automobile insurance, which would ultimately eliminate all of the existing private automobile insurance companies in Manitoba.

Although he was comfortable participating in the caucus and supporting some of its social programs, Desjardins could not support this insurance plan. In response Attorney-General Al Mackling said, "If it means losing Larry we should not proceed with the program."

I disagreed. While I sympathized with Desjardins standing up for his principles, I said the veteran had to understand that the rest of the caucus also had principles. They had a duty to the supporters who had voted for the NDP on the basis that it was committed to fundamental change.

The caucus overwhelmingly supported my position and it was determined that in the next session, legislation would be introduced to create a public automobile insurance program. Shortly after that meeting, Mackling and Pawley came to my office to express their appreciation for my move to keep the party on track.

As a result, the Cabinet soon received the first draft for the public automobile insurance statute as drawn up by the Attorney-General's legislative counsel staff. Two objections were immediately expressed. The first dealt with the title, "Manitoba Government Automobile Insurance." The second focused on the pages of regulatory powers which would enable the Cabinet to operate the plan virtually by regulation with very few legislative constraints.

In my opinion, the use of the word "government" in the title was not appropriate even though Saskatchewan used the same word. I argued that it was necessary to present the plan as a public program, not a government program. More importantly I wanted to underline the philosophy that the government was not an alien source but rather reflected the will of the people through their elected representatives. Schreyer was impressed with the argument and it was agreed that the program's title would be the Manitoba Public Automobile Insurance.

I also suggested that the power to make regulations be limited. The principles of the plan should be specified as much as possible by the statute itself and not by the regulation-making power. This suggestion was also adopted. Those changes removed some of the ammunition which the opposition would have used in its battle against this plan.

The Public Automobile Insurance legislation was introduced for first reading on April 21, 1970 and tabled in the House the following day. The reaction from the opposition and the insurance industry was immediate and predictable.

The nature of the response from the insurance industry was particularly significant. Well aware that the public had little sympathy for large insurance companies, the industry's strategy involved focusing on the plan's impact on independent insurance agents throughout the province. Therefore on April 28th a massive rally was staged on the legislative grounds, as thousands of insurance company employees and agents, who were encouraged to attend, condemned the government plan.

At the same time however, it was apparent that public support for the program was growing in direct proportion to the opposition from the insurance industry. During debate on second reading, which is debate on the principle of the bill, it was standing room only in the public gallery almost every night as almost every MLA spoke at least once on the legislation. The presence of so many people in the chamber was indicative that something important was taking place.

I took aim at comments by Harley Vannon of the Insurance Bureau of Canada, who had suggested that in enacting public automobile insurance, the government was seeking a licence to steal. "How does Mr. Vannon know that?" I asked. "He knows it because he now has the licence and objects to relinquishing it."

To Vannon's suggestion that creating the corporation would result in the elimination of 5,000 jobs, I responded that it was true. It was proof that the government could provide a more effective, efficient and economical program than the existing system.

Throughout debate on second reading there was constant speculation about what would occur when the vote was called. It was a numbers game because with 28 members on the government side and 28 in opposition, the legislature was evenly balanced. The Speaker's vote was required in order to pass the legislation.

On June 24 the vote on second reading was held. Speaker Ben Hanuschak ruled that when the House is equally divided, the Speaker should act in such a way as to permit the matter to proceed. Therefore he voted in favour of the motion and the legislation moved to committee.

The Premier, who was well aware of Desjardins' reluctance to support this legislation, appointed him as chairman of the committee. Because the NDP had a majority in that committee, his vote was not required.

The committee sat for almost five weeks and heard 116 briefs, many of which were highly repetitive. Then the NDP majority in that group ensured its passage and the legislation was sent to the committee of the whole on July 31 in preparation for the third reading stage.

As chairman of the smaller committee Desjardins presented its report and then made a lengthy speech indicating that he could not support a public automobile insurance program. He also singled me out as being the true architect of the plan and the major obstacle to a more reasonable approach. He viewed me as a "frantic fanatic." I did not object to being identified as the culprit who was determined to proceed.

But there was a problem. Without Desjardins' vote the legislation would be defeated. Therefore following his speech, the House was adjourned as the government considered its position. The next few days were frenzied as several emergency meetings were held, including one between Schreyer and Desjardins.

I feared that the government would back down. That fear increased when the Premier finally promised Desjardins to set up a committee to deal with any problems that might arise after the legislation was passed. I was opposed. I argued that, after coming through a very difficult second reading, extended committee meetings and a demonstration, the setting up of such a committee would imply there would be a way to change the program. I said it would be a surrender.

Schreyer, however, convinced the caucus that this proposed committee would not have any real authority to challenge the program. He maintained it would merely remove a psychological barrier to its implementation.

The Premier's strategy was approved. He then made a lengthy speech in the House and set out the following points:

1. The program would proceed.
2. The head office would be based in Brandon.
3. Existing automobile insurance agents would be permitted to sell such insurance at a reduced commission during the lifetime of their agency.

That message seemed to clear the way for Desjardins to support the measure but there was still a problem. A vote was required to move the legislation out of committee of the whole to the third reading stage but the NDP lacked a majority. In committee of the whole the Speaker is not in the chair and traditionally does not sit in the chamber. This left the government with 28 members, one of whom was chairman. Without Hanuschak sitting as an MLA the motion could be defeated.

I, however, believed that the Speaker was still an MLA and broached the matter with Hanuschak. As a loyal New Democrat who had fought for public automobile insurance, I said it would be inexplicable to his constituents if the plan was defeated because Hanuschak had not voted. Therefore I asked that, as a signal to the media and the Opposition, Hanuschak occupy the seat designated for him as an MLA, while the committee was considering other matters prior to the vote on the contentious legislation.

At the next meeting of the committee of the whole, Hanuschak unexpectedly entered the chamber and sat in his seat. The message was clear. The prospect of an evenly divided vote was laid to rest.

Ultimately Hanuschak was not required to vote. Gordon Beard, the Independent MLA for Churchill, voted in favour of receiving the committee report and the legislation moved to the next stage, third reading.

In mid-August 1970, public automobile insurance passed the last hurdle and became law. It marked a major change in the economic structure of Manitoba.

Ultimately events proved that Schreyer's course of action was correct. The special committee set up to ease Desjardins' concerns caused no problems. One reason for that result may have been the appointment of party president Murdoch MacKay to the committee, something I had proposed. MacKay ensured that no attempt was made to inhibit implementation of the program or interfere with any of its fundamental principles.

Schreyer was also correct in permitting the agents to continue writing policies and licensing drivers. This is one of the best features of the public automobile insurance program.

A Manitoban can buy a car and within minutes go to an agent and obtain licence plates and automobile insurance without having to go through any of the usual government bureaucracy. I had never anticipated such a result. It came about more by compromise and accident than by any brilliant planning on the part of the government.

The debate on automobile insurance and its aftermath resulted in two interesting developments. One involved the Opposition which saw an opportunity to divide the government by pitting Schreyer against me, arguing that I rather than the Premier was the power in the NDP government.

During debate on automobile insurance Liberal Gil Molgat was quite explicit on this point. Noting that Schreyer had been elected leader of the NDP he said, "The luckiest thing that ever happened to the NDP was that Green was not chosen as its leader."

When Molgat finished, I asked whether he would permit a question. Noting Molgat's reference to myself, I said, "You have said that the luckiest thing that ever happened to the NDP is that I was not chosen as its leader. I will let that pass without comment. Will the member agree that the second luckiest thing that ever happened to the NDP is that he, Molgat, had been the leader of the Liberal party?"

The second event occurred at a cabinet meeting when Schreyer asked whether the ministers had any objection to a by-election in St. Boniface. He indicated that Desjardins, who was feeling badly about the situation he had been placed in, wanted to obtain the approval of his constituents.

I objected to a by-election in St. Boniface. I suggested that Desjardins wanted to campaign in St. Boniface on the promise to protect Schreyer from Green. But if that was what the cabinet wanted I would resign and request a by-election in Inkster at the same time. I would then campaign in Inkster on the promise to protect Schreyer from Desjardins. The subject of by-elections was immediately dropped.

Public automobile insurance came into effect on September 21, 1970. It was an immediate political and economic success. Over the years there have been changes to the program but it has become part of the fabric of Manitoba.

When the Conservatives came to power in 1977, Premier Sterling Lyon met with the insurance industry representatives from eastern Canada. I rose in the House and said the insurance representatives from Toronto should be made aware that a future NDP would undo any restoration of private automobile insurance in the province. Borrowing rhetoric from Israeli General Moshe Dayan, I warned the industry not to unpack their bags because the road from Toronto to Winnipeg was also the road from Winnipeg to Toronto.

PUBLIC AID TO PRIVATE SCHOOLS

When Manitoba became a province, the school system, as in several other jurisdictions, was entirely denominational. For the most part the French population was serviced by Roman Catholic French schools and the English population by the Protestant school system. When English became the dominant language in the province, a publicly-funded school system was established.

The Manitoba Act had specified that the existence of the denominational schools could continue, but did not guarantee public financing. The French Catholic system regarded this as a betrayal. It argued with some justification that the public school system was essentially a Protestant system which would be funded by everybody while the Catholics would not only fund the public system but, if they wanted their own system, would be required to finance that as well.

With considerable financial sacrifice by supporters, the Catholic system continued to exist. Over the years it was joined by other private schools, both religious and secular. They too were funded by those who utilized them, while public schools were supported by general taxation, for the most part levied against real property.

When real property financing began to pay for less and less of the school system expenses, the province was urged to subsidize the school system through general taxation. This was a progressive development.

Over the years the French Catholic system expressed a grievance, claiming its schools had been dealt with unjustly and the spirit, if not the legal requirements, of the Manitoba Act had been violated.

When Larry Desjardins was elected to Manitoba Legislature in 1959 he became an articulate and forceful champion of the French Catholic system. At that time Duff Roblin was the Premier. Fluently bilingual, he was sympathetic to the plight of the private school system. His difficulty lay within his own caucus. For instance, Fred Groves, the member for St. Vital, was adamantly opposed to any funding for private schools, a position which probably had the support of the majority of the electorate in Manitoba.

Nevertheless, in the early 1960s, Roblin with the assistance of key legal advisor Maurice Arpin, developed a program. This shared-services program maintained the principle of not providing aid to private schools, but proposed a method whereby private schools and their students could avail themselves of services provided in the public schools. For instance, private school students would be entitled to obtain the same books provided to public schools at the expense of the Government. In addition public school gymnasiums could be made available on a shared service basis to private schools.

The introduction of this program became an issue within the NDP. I was chosen to head a policy committee to formulate a policy with respect to shared services and the general issue of public aid to private schools. The committee subsequently came out with a statement which essentially concluded no public taxpayers' money should be used to finance the private school system. The basic reason was that public tax revenue should not be used for the propagation of any religious or other beliefs.

As a result, when the shared-services program was introduced, it was opposed by almost all New Democrats, including Russ Paulley and Saul Cherniack. The lone dissenter was Ed Schreyer who publicly expressed support for some public funding of private schools, particularly the shared-services program. Paulley and Cherniack regarded that position as a breach of caucus solidarity and a departure from what was regarded as a longstanding NDP position. Nevertheless the program came into effect and was functioning when the NDP came to power.

Adhering to his earlier position, Schreyer indicated his administration would do something with regard to the private school grievance. That public statement about some form of assistance was like laying down a gauntlet to myself and other New Democrats, who opposed any such program.

I wrote a public letter to the Premier, indicating I could not support public aid to private schools. When this letter was made public on March 15, 1971 debate within the party was inevitable.

I was supported by many traditional New Democrats, some of whom had supported Schreyer in the leadership campaign. Indeed some believed this debate was a renewal of that race. I denied it, insisting I had been forced into publicly opposing the Premier's position because it was contrary to everything I had espoused in regard to this issue.

Resentment of Schreyer's position became apparent at a party convention in Brandon in November 1971. Those opposed to the proposal intended to bring the matter to a head. A resolution prepared by the Thompson constituency organization was presented by Wilf Hudson of the United Steel Workers of America.

I believed the resolution would be approved and create a severe rupture within the party and the government. Therefore I took the floor, indicating my opposition to public financing of private schools but also indicating that one could have the opposite view and still be a loyal New Democrat.

I said that whether or not the government should provide public aid to private schools is an issue of personal conscience and not one on which there should be a party policy. I had previously regarded the issue as one of party policy. Nevertheless at my urging, no vote was held on the resolution and it was generally accepted that this issue would be regarded as a matter of personal conscience for each member of the Legislature.

The tabling of the resolution had a strange public impact. The *Winnipeg Tribune* wrote an editorial which suggested that Schreyer was in total control of the NDP and had forced people such as myself to follow his wishes. Recognizing the unfairness and danger in the editorial, Schreyer immediately held a news conference where he disowned what had been written in the editorial.

The *Tribune* ignored the news conference, thus prompting me to resort to a tactic which I had developed and used repeatedly in dealing with the press. I purchased an advertisement in the *Tribune*. It stated:

> "For some time now I have watched the Editorial Page of the Winnipeg Tribune attempting to make it appear that the Cabinet of Manitoba has within it serious divisions as to the Government's general policy directions.
>
> Most often these attempts have taken the form of vague references to "radicals in the Cabinet." However, more recently the Tribune, in an editorial became more specific and identified the "Greens" as somehow representing the faction Mr. Schreyer has to drag along by the scruff of the neck.
>
> I have made it a long standing rule in my political life to never complain about the treatment afforded to me by the press. Nor have I expected political endorsation of either my or the New Democratic Party's views. I have always held the view that the press is a very important element in the political process.
>
> Therefore, although I make no criticism of the Tribune for its editorial, I feel that I should point out that the Winnipeg Tribune is not attempting to help Mr. Schreyer, the Government or the New

Democratic Party. Its purpose is rather to make things difficult for Mr. Schreyer, the Government, and the New Democratic Party. In pursuing this purpose, and attempting to score points by suggesting that somehow I am at odds with the Government, it ignores the following facts which are well-known.

When I was in opposition during 1966-1969 and during the 1969 campaign, I concentrated my efforts on these main areas:

a) the reduction of premium taxes in favour of ability to pay taxes.

b) the need for a public automobile insurance program.

c) the organization of government services in greater Winnipeg under one municipal government.

d) a review of the South Indian Lake High Level Diversion project.

e) the elimination of discriminatory injunctions against employees.

f) the elimination of secrecy with respect to the Manitoba Development Fund.

The Tribune can refer to Hansard in the years of 1966-1969 to see how my comments on these subjects compare with present Government policy. It should be obvious to its readers that the major thrust of our Government's program has followed exactly the points which I concentrated upon in opposition and during the election campaign. To try to set me up as a dissident within the Government is ludicrous and illustrates the lengths to which the Tribune will go to try to make trouble for the Government.

This letter is therefore sent in the hope that Citizens of Manitoba will have a better perspective of the credibility of the editorial page of the Winnipeg Tribune.

A further measure of its credibility can be deduced from the following facts:

a) The Tribune decided not to comment on Mr. Schreyer's Press Conference of last Friday, which I am therefore having printed at personal expense by the purchase of this advertisement.

b) on August 27th, 1970, a Tribune reporter, Mr. Gary Scherbain, reserved an hour and one-half of my time for the purpose of obtaining a taped interview so that a portrait of Sid Green could appear in this paper. That portrait was never printed, presumably because it would not have helped the Tribune in its attempt to create trouble for the Government.

If the Winnipeg Tribune was truly interested in showing its readers what a problem I am to Mr. Schreyer, why does it not now print the material which it took my time to assemble."

Tom Green, the editor of the *Winnipeg Tribune*, was furious with the advertisement. He called me and indicated reporters were not required to report every innocuous statement made by the Premier. As well, he suggested that the Premier involved in dispute with one of his cabinet ministers did not constitute news. He did however, indicate my advertisement would be published without charge. Since I was seeking financial support, I said I was quite willing to have the *Tribune* contribute to the cost. The editor angrily cut off the discussion and I was sent a bill without a contribution from the *Tribune*.

In the next few months it became apparent Schreyer had requested the administration to develop a policy and program for the provision of public aid to private schools. There was no debate or decision on the subject because he had taken action without discussion in cabinet. When it became apparent this process was taking place I was compelled to make a decision. The program was going to be implemented and I did not intend to see this happen without some debate. I could not be a member of the cabinet and conduct a debate with the Premier.

On March 2, 1972 I forwarded a letter to the Premier. The crucial paragraph stated:

> "As a result of the failure to resolve this issue and as a result
> of the developments indicated, I am convinced that my position
> in the Executive Council prevents me from properly representing
> my constituency. I accordingly hereby resign from the Executive
> Council and from all positions which I hold in connection
> therewith."

The resignation was of course a thunderbolt. Schreyer could not back down and I had burned my bridges. As Schreyer told Herb Schultz, "Green shouldn't threaten to resign." Then he corrected himself, "He didn't threaten. He resigned."

A public debate was inevitable and those in cabinet who were normally opposed to public aid were furious. With me as the champion of what had been their position, they now were reluctant to support it. Meanwhile I began working with a committee which repeatedly published a constantly growing advertisement, containing the names of those who opposed the Government's position on public aid to private schools.

The anti-public aid position rapidly gained momentum. Finally, before the 1972 session began, Schreyer announced that instead of bringing in legislation, he would introduce a private member's resolution which would be sufficiently ambiguously worded to enable a positive vote. Ultimately he presented a lengthy resolution with preambles outlining his version of historical matters and ending with the following:

"THEREFORE BE IT RESOLVED that a special Committee of the Legislature be appointed to consider and recommend on proposals submitted in the reference paper on options for greater community and parental involvement within the public school system and which also includes the concept of accommodating those private and denominational schools that may desire to integrate into the public schools; the advisability of revising the programme of shared services and assistance to students of private schools in the light of the report of the earlier Special Committees of 1964, and because of the anomalies discovered in the actual operation of legislation governing shared services since 1966 as shown in the statistical and contract form appendices in the above noted submitted reference paper; the legislation adopted in 1967 in the provinces of Alberta and Saskatchewan; changes enacted in Ontario in 1972 and such other documents and information as may, from time to time, be laid before it;

AND BE IT FURTHER RESOLVED that this Special Committee have power to sit during the present session and in the recess after prorogation and to submit a report, with recommendations to this House or any or all of the alternatives hereby referred to it.

Considerable discussion occurred about what the resolution meant. Pro-public aid people, including Desjardins, said passing the resolution would constitute a legislative direction, enabling the government to go ahead. Anti-public aid people said the resolution was simply an expression of opinion which did not call for the actual provision of public aid.

When I left cabinet I continued as a member of the NDP caucus. A strong supporter of the Government positions, I participated fully in the debates on the Throne speech and budget. In particular, I supported the Government on the Nelson River Development, which was under Schreyer's jurisdiction.

I was also a paid policy consultant for the caucus. As a consultant I was responsible for developing several seminars which received considerable attention. One, which dealt with the economy, was held at the University of Manitoba and was addressed by John Crispo and Reuben Bellan. Another involved a four-day railway trip to Thompson which included seminars along the way and various whistle stops.

Meanwhile the momentum supporting my position on school funding increased. More and more New Democrats were voicing their opposition to public aid for private schools. But at this time I learned that Saul Miller and Schreyer had devised a system whereby private schools could become part of the public system while maintaining their private character. In other words they planned to achieve through administrative action what was being sought on the basis of principle in the Legislature. This action made the debate irrelevant and I felt completely defeated. Despite my objections, public aid to private schools would occur.

Not only had I failed to prevent the program but I had taken himself out of the cabinet and left power in the hands of those glad to see me go. Realizing the futility of my position, I announced in the House that the debate concerning private schools was no longer of the same consequence as it had been when I resigned from the cabinet. I was willing to serve in any position that the Premier wished to place me.

Immediately Schreyer told me I would be welcomed back into cabinet. I urged him to act quickly or detractors would convince him to the contrary. And that is exactly what happened. Several ministers, particularly Miller and Paulley, who had been embarrassed by the entire process, strongly objected to my return to cabinet. They told the Premier to wait until the legislative debate was concluded.

Perhaps they felt that my position in the Legislature would change if I was kept out of the cabinet. Regardless of the reason, Schreyer reluctantly told me that any reinstatement would have to wait.

Withholding of the cabinet post did nothing to deter me from my position with respect to the debate on public aid to private to schools. I conducted it with the same intensity as I had before announcing my willingness to return to cabinet. But I did learn something from the process – my detractors, namely Miller, Cherniack and Paulley would go to any lengths to try to minimize my influence in cabinet. This attitude would have significant implications on the future of my political career.

When Schreyer was interviewed about his resolution, he indicated a willingness to compromise. He suggested that I also compromise. When approached by the media, I responded, "Schreyer and I are both in Winnipeg. He wants to go east to Halifax and I want to go west to Vancouver. He says that a compromise is for us to go to Toronto."

The actual content of the resolution was clarified when it was formally introduced. Schreyer said it was intended to be a vehicle to enable the funding of private schools. The extent of such funding would be a matter of development and consideration.

The Premier urged the members of the Legislature to set aside emotion and make a rational decision on the subject. Yet, while asking MLAs to deal with the matter unemotionally, he referred to the Roman Catholic schools' grievance as a "festering sore" on the landscape of Manitoba.

Insisting his own position was entirely based on logic, rather than emotion, he said on several occasions, "The logic that lies beneath the concept of shared services is irrefutable in every respect... The logic is pristine, pure and irrefutable" (Hansard 19, 1972) When Schreyer concluded, I adjourned debate. Members of the Legislature regarded me as the most public spokesman on the subject and agreed I was entitled to make the first speech against the proposal.

But Russ Paulley, who had been appointed House Leader when I resigned, wanted to make my presentation as innocuous as possible. Although a fierce opponent to public aid for private schools he ultimately voted with Schreyer on the resolution. For the moment, as House Leader he determined when debate on the subject would be called. He called the debate at 5:00 p.m. on Thursday afternoon,a time when the media had left the gallery. His ploy failed. As soon as debate was called, the media rushed back to the press gallery.

I spoke from 5:00 to 5:30. The House then adjourned and resumed that evening. Accepting Schreyer's challenge to discuss the issue on a rational rather than an emotional basis, I dealt with the question of separation of church and state and the necessity of maintaining a strong public school system. I agreed that the public school system had defects but maintained the encouragement of a private system would inevitably hurt the public school system.

I perceived my greatest difficulty would be convincing my own caucus that my stand on the public school issue was not a resurrection of the leadership race. The school aid question was one which I had advocated for many years and could not abandon. In conclusion I quoted Shakespeare's Polonius: "And this above all, to thine own self be true, and it must follow, as the night the day, thou can'st not then be false to any man."

The press gallery was very attentive when I spoke, and on the whole the speech was well received. In particular, Cyrille Felteau, a reporter from the Quebec newspaper *La Presse*, wrote:

> "During my stay in Winnipeg, I had the good fortune to hear Sidney Green explain to the legislature the basis of his views on this profound question that resonates through the politics and history of the province.
>
> I say 'good fortune' because his speech, which was classical in its eloquence, was an event in itself.
>
> A respectful silence reigned during his speech of over an hour, which I rank as among the most powerful that I have ever heard in a parliamentary chamber."

The debate continued, with opposition members voicing their disagreement with the resolution. Many, particularly Conservative Leader Sidney Spivak, also tried to use the debate to embarrass Schreyer.

The vote on the resolution was held on the last day of the session. Thirty MLAs voted against the resolution while 22 supported it. Of those opposing it, 12 were New Democrats who wanted to maintain their opposition to public aid to private schools. On the other hand Miller, Cherniack and Paulley abandoned the principles they had advocated throughout their political lives and supported the Premier.

Immediately after the vote, Schreyer asked me if I was prepared to be sworn in as a minister. I agreed and the swearing in occurred very quickly. In doing this, Schreyer denied my detractors another chance to keep me out of the Cabinet. I was sworn in as Minister of Mines and Natural Resources in a private ceremony and resumed my position as House Leader.

For all intents and purposes I had won the debate on whether the Government would enact legislation to provide public aid to private and parochial schools. In the end, however, the war was lost. Schreyer and Miller proceeded to make administrative arrangements with certain private schools, allowing them to become part of the public system and therefore obtain effective public funding.

At this stage there was nothing I could do. Another resignation from Cabinet would not reverse the trend and would result in loss of power and influence. Since I had worked hard and long to obtain political power, I knew at this stage a move against public aid to private schools would be futile.

Over the next years the principle of no public aid to private schools was encroached on a regular basis by the department of education. When the Conservatives came to power in 1977 they formally introduced legislation and administrative procedures to continue and expand the aid provided by the Schreyer government. Now in opposition, the New Democrats could hardly object. They had opened the floodgates. Public aid to private and parochial schools would become a feature of the Manitoba social and economic system.

The results I predicted are apparent. An increasing number of parents, who naturally want their children to get a good education, are giving up on the public system and sending their children to private schools. The opportunity to send them to private schools increases with increasing government aid.

Those who send their children to private schools lose interest in the public system which becomes a residual system available to those who can't afford anything better. The enhancement of the private system, along with the deterioration of the public system, has a leapfrogging effect. It appears that little can be done at present to reverse the process.

Manitoba is becoming a province where the school system is based on religious and ethnic background. This is in keeping with present political correctness whereby political parties are encouraged to deal with people as part of ethnic communities rather than as individuals.

The Progressive Party later opposed this trend to no avail. Ultimately it can only have a negative effect on the rights of individuals within the province of Manitoba. The NDP cannot absolve itself of responsibility for this development.

TRADE UNIONISM AND LABOUR LAWS

In addition to fulfilling major election promises, I was determined to achieve certain objectives in labour relations.

My interest in labour laws began when, in the early 1940s, I was employed at Oretski's Department store on Selkirk Avenue in north Winnipeg. Employees at the store worked six days a week, including a 10-hour shift on Saturdays which did not end until 10:00 p.m.

Because most of the employees were teenagers, Saturday night was a special time, especially in the summer when many would take the "Moonlight" train to Winnipeg Beach. But the 10 p.m. closing made such a trip impossible. They were also upset about wages which ranged from $9 to $12 a week.

As a result the workers organized and ultimately went on strike. One request was the right to end work at 6:00 p.m. on Saturdays. After I and fellow workers walked the picket line for several days, the strike was settled with some of the demands being met, but the Saturday night shift was reduced by only one hour so the "Moonlight" trip was still out.

That event made an impression on me and affected what I did as a lawyer. By the time I was associated with Leon Mitchell, I had become prominent in the field of labour law and the trade union movement, particularly in cases which involved injunctions restraining the right of workers to picket.

In a case where a trade union and its members were prohibited from engaging in what was alleged to be an unlawful strike, I argued that an injunction to restrain a work stoppage was in fact, an injunction to enforce the performance of personal services. But, I noted it was a well established principle of the English common law that a court could not enforce the performance of personal services. In my view, the same principle applied to employees who collectively refused to perform work. I also argued that the ultimate result of an injunction to bring an employee back to work was that a sheriff would have to stand over the employee with a whip to ensure the court order was obeyed. The law in effect, enforced mandatory labour.

While I was only moderately successful in cases involving both picketing and back-to-work injunctions, I did receive support from trade unions which employed me to argue many cases. I also lectured in labour to trade union officials and was ultimately employed by the Manitoba Law school as a labour law lecturer.

Despite the support which I received from the trade union movement when I was arguing on their behalf, from the outset it was apparent that my views in regard to labour laws did not conform to traditional trade union demands.

The unions wanted more favorable laws, such as changes to the Labour Relations Act in order to make it easier for unions to organize. I however, argued that there were only two major principles upon which trade unions could advance their position. The first was the right to engage in collective bargaining, which implied the right to withdraw their services if they were not able to conclude a satisfying collective agreement.

The second was the right to appeal to the public and other workers for support when engaged in a labour dispute. This appeal involved the right to peacefully parade around the work place and any other area which they felt would be advantageous. This conduct was commonly known as picketing and the laws in Canada were very restrictive in regard to such action.

I argued that the same laws that applied to people demonstrating against furriers for killing wild animals should be applicable to employees who were engaged in what they considered to be a fair fight with their employers. I demonstrated that it was only when unions were concerned that peaceful demonstrations were outlawed and judges took it upon themselves to order the performance of personal services.

In other words, I urged that unions receive equal treatment rather than special treatment. I advocated the elimination of all laws which restricted employees from collectively withdrawing their services and called for the repeal of laws which made it illegal for employees to demonstrate for popular support.

When the NDP became government, at my instigation, the Labour Relations Act was changed to remove most of the restrictions to the right of a trade union and employees to bargain collectively and withdraw labour in support of negotiations for better terms and conditions of employment.

The most significant change came with respect to injunctions. I wanted the general laws of Manitoba changed so that employees would no longer be prevented from peaceful expressions of opinion – picket – and to eliminate back-to-work orders by courts. I emphasized that these were not labour laws and should not be included in the Labour Act. Accordingly, amendments to the Queen's Bench Act were passed which changed the general law with two major stipulations: no injunction would be granted to restrain peaceful picketing and no injunction would be granted which would require a person to go to work or go to jail.

When this amendment was introduced, Opposition MLAs who were aware of my background in labour relations, predicted that the changes would result in violence. After 30 years there has been no suggestion that any violence took place because of what has been called the "Green amendment."

Instead courts have not restrained workers from expressing their opinions and no judges have ordered workers to work. For many years Manitoba was the only jurisdiction in North America which guaranteed freedom of expression to employees to engage in public demonstrations and prohibited courts from giving back-to-work orders.

It is significant that in 1999 the Supreme Court of Canada considered a case where the employees had been prevented by a judge from engaging in peaceful picketing. The case involved a challenge to laws which prevented secondary boycotts on the grounds that they constituted an infringement on freedom of speech as guaranteed by the Charter of Rights and Freedoms. The Supreme Court ruled against the injunction and granted the rights to the employees on the same basis as the "Green amendment." The Manitoba government's establishment of this right preceded the Supreme Court's decision by almost thirty years.

As a union lawyer and later as a member of the legislature, I had been adamantly opposed to 'back to work' legislation. Such legislation was usually enacted with reference to strikes which were deemed to affect the public interest, such as railroads and hospitals. My own view was, that although the employer was entitled to the right to maintain its services during a strike, the question as to whether or not the dispute should be resolved, should be left with collective bargaining and should not be determined by 'back to work' provisions imposed by the legislature. No 'back to work' legislation was enacted by the NDP government between 1969 and 1977. I take responsibility for having prevented it.

In 1976 there was a transit strike in Winnipeg. The City of Winnipeg requested the NDP government to enact 'back to work' legislation. After the strike had lasted for several months a startling event took place. At the opening of the legislative session on March 8, 1976. Mayor Steven Juba was present in the visitors section. Labour Minister Russ Paulley, without consulting caucus or cabinet, announced that he would be introducing 'back to work' legislation. I rose to my feet and said that I could not support such legislation. I received the support of the NDP caucus and cabinet. Mayor Juba told City Council. Within several days the strike was settled by free collective bargaining. This is the only instance in parliamentary history of which I am aware where one cabinet minister rises in Chambers and makes an official announcement indicating that the government is going to do something and another cabinet ministers gets up and says what the first cabinet minister would be done would not be done.

Ironically I, who was a trade union favourite between 1966 and 1973, was later viewed as Public Enemy Number One by the unions. The change occurred in the mid-70's when trade unions, which had not succeeded in many disputes, started to pressure the government to pass laws which would make special provisions that discriminated in favour of trade union organizations.

These measures included first-agreement contract legislation which imposed a collective agreement when the employer and employees were unable to reach one. Such legislation was anathema to me. I insisted on maintaining the principle of free collective bargaining, where both the employer and employees had the right to refuse to enter into an agreement.

The unions also pushed for laws prohibiting employers from hiring substitute workers if their own people refused to work. This was contrary to the principles of free collective bargaining, a cornerstone of my argument.

Through the years my position on trade unionism and labour laws remained the same, but what had been praised was ultimately condemned.

UNIFICATION OF GREATER WINNIPEG

Since the creation of Metro government in the early 1960's, municipal politics in Manitoba had been in a turmoil. Metro was superimposed over 13 municipalities, each with a mayor, council and administration, including separate police forces and fire departments. Metro councillors were directly elected by the people but the chairman was appointed by the provincial government.

Metro government was responsible for Greater Winnipeg services, such as transit, sewer and water, major roads, parks and planning. Because these services had been largely under the control of municipal governments, any planning was very complicated.

Metro council became responsible for many of the services which had been traditionally within the jurisdiction of municipal governments which led to inevitable conflict between the two levels. Specifically the municipal governments now had another group to blame for most of the problems which they could not resolve.

They also took aim at Metro government for purely political reasons. The majority of municipal councils and their mayors were quite happy that Metro existed. It was a perfect scapegoat.

The Metropolitan Corporation collected its entire revenue from the municipalities. Since more than 50 percent of those revenues came from the City of Winnipeg property and business taxes, the suburban municipalities were receiving a benefit financed by other parts of the city. For instance, if one of their streets became a Metro road, the municipality was relieved of spending money to maintain the road, while the citizens of Winnipeg bore the cost.

In other words, the municipalities could have their cake and eat it too. They could complain about Metro government but at the same time reap the benefits. The exception was the City of Winnipeg. Despite the fact that

Winnipeg also benefited if its streets were placed under Metro jurisdiction, just as it had benefited when it was determined that the Assiniboine and Kildonan Parks would be funded by Greater Winnipeg, the Winnipeg Council resisted Metro encroachments.

Winnipeg Mayor Steve Juba repeatedly attacked Metro and tried to retain Winnipeg jurisdiction over all of its existing services. With city engineer Bill Hurst, he demanded that Winnipeg streets not be designated as major metro streets even though they fit the criteria

Juba maintained Metro was so inefficient that Winnipeg would save money even if it bore the entire cost of a road rather than allow the other level of government to do so. This battle and others continued throughout the existence of Metro.

When I was a Metro councillor between 1962 and 1966, I argued that the City of Winnipeg should be amalgamated. I also introduced a motion calling for the chairman of Metro to be elected rather than appointed by the provincial government. Eventually this came to pass. Through ingenious manipulation by Councillor Peter Tarasko, Lawrence Ostrander became the first elected Metro chairman, on the understanding that he would not run for re-election after one term. He kept his promise and subsequently Jack Willis was elected by fellow councillors as chairman. Willis continued to be Metro chairman until its demise in 1972.

When I became an Opposition MLA, I continued to pursue the unification of greater Winnipeg. I met with resistance from fellow-New Democrat Saul Miller. The former mayor of West Kildonan was adamantly opposed to amalgamation.

On the other hand Saul Cherniack and most of the other MLAs had spoken in favour of amalgamation for many years and were committed to the process. The municipal wing of the New Democratic Party had pursued amalgamation but that group was composed largely of aldermen and school trustees in Winnipeg. Those from the suburban municipalities, such as Miller and Al Mackling, who was an alderman in St.James, were adamantly opposed to any change in the structure.

The matter was brought to a head at the 1968 convention when a resolution in favour of amalgamating was considered. Following a debate and attempts to prevent a vote, the delegates eventually voted overwhelmingly in favor of the resolution and the unification of greater Winnipeg became party policy before the 1969 election.

A harbinger of the difficulties that would be encountered in the NDP caucus relative to the unification of the City of Greater Winnipeg came during the last three days of the election campaign. Although most party diehards, including Saul Cherniak and Saul Miller, regarded it as NDP sacred scroll, that policy was made at convention. Ed Schreyer was apparently not wedded to this principle.

On the Friday before the election Schreyer made a statement which indicated the party would not seek the amalgamation of greater Winnipeg but would rather divide the City into six regions. He had apparently discussed this policy with Mackling and perhaps Miller. I was furious. Those who had said I was trying to be a dictator were now going against their professed views and completely ignoring a party position.

Schreyer made the statement without any notice or consultation with me. When I read the statement in the newspaper on Saturday evening I immediately called Schreyer. Expressing my displeasure I indicated that I did not intend to abandon my position which had been adopted as a party policy. Because only three days remained until the vote, I did not intend to disrupt the campaign. I made my position clear but Schreyer maintained that his press release was a sensible compromise.

After medicare premiums were reduced and public automobile insurance was introduced, I turned to the unification issue. I believed it should be the next major undertaking for the New Democratic Party. The majority of elected representatives who had supported the concept in the past, continued their support while others were more reluctant. Nevertheless the decision was made to proceed.

The acquiescence of both Miller and Mackling was obtained. In order to make the pill easier to swallow, Mackling was appointed chairman of a committee to design a program which could be translated into legislation.

The plan was further advanced by the hiring of Meyer Brownstone, formerly a high-level civil servant in Saskatchewan's CCF government. He came to Winnipeg from Toronto with the mandate of implementing the program. Brownstone and a caucus committee began protracted discussions about how the goals could be achieved.

At the NDP annual convention that fall, however, no mention was made about amalgamation. I began to suspect that Mackling was dragging his feet in order to ensure the program would not be implemented. Therefore I raised the issue again in cabinet and urgently demanded that the next session contain legislation to unify the municipalities of greater Winnipeg.

However the committee which was supposed to work on the subject had not made sufficient progress to prepare draft legislation. It appeared that my goal would not be achieved.

Fortuitously I received a memorandum from Earl Levin, the director of planning for the Metropolitan Corporation and an advocate of amalgamation. He and Juba were bitter enemies. Nevertheless Levin prepared a memo which basically suggested that the City of Winnipeg could be divided into six administrative districts which would be run by six committees composed of councillors elected from the areas concerned.

While the memo was intended to be a plan for the future City of Winnipeg, it would have required considerable administrative and legislative changes. But I believed this plan would provide a bridge from the existing administration of the thirteen municipalities and Metro to an administration involving one unified city.

Using Levin's memo as a basis, I prepared my own memo for cabinet, recommending unification. Tax unity would commence immediately to ensure that all people within Greater Winnipeg would pay taxes to a central authority. But instead of having a central authority administer the services, I suggested the establishment of 13 community committees, composed of councillors who had been elected in the areas of the pre-existing municipal governments.

This would mean no significant administrative change. Instead the municipalities would continue to administer the same services they had previously administered. They would do so through a committee of councillors who, while part of the Greater Winnipeg council, would in effect, be the administrators of services within their areas.

This plan would enable quick passage of the legislation while the ultimate administration of the City of Winnipeg would depend on how the new council proceeded.

The memo was discussed by cabinet and despite misgivings expressed by Mackling and Miller, was approved. It was agreed that legislation based on the memorandum would be drafted by the committee of urban affairs.

Meanwhile, Cherniack replaced Mackling as chairman of the committee and agreed to implement the program for the 1971 legislative session. He immediately set to work with Meyer Brownstone and hired journalist Ellen Simmons to prepare a white paper which would form the basis for discussion at a series of meetings throughout Greater Winnipeg.

I was out of the city when the document was prepared but it translated what I regarded as a makeshift expedient into a revolutionary new type of municipal government. The proposal essentially detailed a centralized financial system with a totally decentralized administration, involving community committees and a new concept, resident advisory groups.

The white paper was heralded as a major breakthrough in municipal government which would satisfy both those who wanted more centralization and those who favored decentralization.

By the time I returned to Winnipeg, meetings concerning the new proposal were already underway. I was asked to participate in some meetings where he was active in answering criticism from those who wanted to retain the existing system.

At a meeting involving the municipalities of Tuxedo and Fort Garry I did not try to convince people of the correctness of the government position. As a matter of fact I had little faith in the philosophical arguments with respect to the revolutionary new form of municipal government and stayed away from that topic completely.

Instead I concentrated on the need for a reorganization of Greater Winnipeg in order to remove the unfair burden of taxes on those in the core area for the benefit of the more affluent who lived in municipalities surrounding the City.

I did not expect to convert those opposed to amalgamation but did attempt to expose their specious arguments. For instance at one meeting, a person suggested that the amalgamation proposal amounted to a form of communism. I responded by indicating that the person had identified people such as Winnipeg Mayor Steve Juba, Liberal Charles Huband and many other distinguished citizens as communists. I said the questioner had converted more people to communism than Joseph Stalin had ever hoped for.

Although my response did not win any support from those who opposed amalgamation it solidified the position of those in favor of a change.

Prior to the session the government faced two by-elections, one of which was in St. Vital, a municipality within Greater Winnipeg. The amalgamation issue was prominent in that race, which was won by the NDP candidate Jim Walding. Another New Democrat, Pete Adam, was elected in the Ste. Rose by-election.

At the next legislative session a bitter debate ensued over the unification of Greater Winnipeg and, as with the Autopac debate, the public galleries were filled night after night.

One major change which occurred during debate affected the way in which the mayor is elected. In the original proposal the mayor was to be elected by the councillors. I and others felt this proposal was designed specifically to eliminate the possibility of Juba becoming mayor. This was unfair for practical and other reasons. After all, Juba had been the most effective spokesman for unification. To deny him the right to run as mayor seemed to be an unfitting reward for his work.

Secondly the entire proposal gave tremendous power to the councillors who would be elected from various wards and whose duties would involve extensive administration of the areas where they had been elected. There was no mechanism within the new structure which ensured an over-all view of the City.

Given the propaganda which had gone into the concept and the suggested desirability of total decentralization, I believed the only possibility for such a mechanism was a mayoralty election where citizens of every part of the City spoke as a whole.

Again there was a dispute in caucus about the matter. Miller and Cherniack led the fight to retain the non-elected mayor, while Schreyer and I advocated the change. Those in favor of an elected mayor won and the legislation was changed. The mayor of Winnipeg would be elected by all citizens rather than by councillors.

Eventually the legislation was passed. On December 31, 1971 there were 13 municipalities and a Metro government administering the City of Winnipeg. On January 1, 1972 the City of Winnipeg came under the jurisdiction of one council. A civic election was held in the fall of 1971. Fifty councillors were elected. Juba easily defeated Metro chairman Jack Willis and became the first mayor of the unified City of Winnipeg.

After the legislation was passed I became the Minister of Urban Affairs. I would have preferred to have Levin, whom I regarded as the architect of the system, as his deputy minister. However because Levin was disliked by Juba, members of the cabinet felt that it would be impolitic to appoint him. I relented and chose a respected member of the Metro administration, Andrew Curry.

In various statements I made it clear that he was not wedded to the council system as legislated and fully expected that it would be transitional. It was designed to provide an effective way of moving from 13 municipalities to one and its ultimate structure would depend on the wishes of the newly established council.

Much to the chagrin of those who viewed the new form of government as ideal, Winnipeg City Council continued to seek changes to the Statute. For instance the City sought and achieved a reduction in the size of council. At present it consists of 15 councillors and an elected mayor. This is the model that I expected would eventually occur.

The creation of Unicity was another platform achievement of the New Democratic Party that did not involve any public expenditure and achieved greater efficiency for municipal government in Manitoba.

THE PAS FORESTRY COMPLEX

Prior to the 1966 election the Roblin government announced a prized mega-project: a multinational corporation was going to build a forestry complex at The Pas, Manitoba, involving an investment of some $90 million.

Details of the investors were sparse, but they involved Technopulp Inc., a corporation owned by Europeans with an office in New Jersey. In return for building a pulp mill, lumber mill and support facilities close to The Pas, the conglomerate was to receive timber cutting rights over a large portion of northwestern Manitoba. The government heralded the deal as a major achievement bringing high-paying jobs and industrial development to the North.

After the election, the Opposition sought further information about the project. The major breakthrough occurred when Saul Cherniack obtained information about a debenture registered in the Land Titles Office which indicated that the Manitoba Development Corporation (Manitoba Development Fund at that time) was lending money to the complex entrepreneurs at a very favourable interest rate.

With that information the Opposition stepped up its attack. While Premier Duff Roblin maintained he had negotiated a very good deal for the Province, I compared the negotiations to the sale of Manhattan. The Indians returning to their teepees rubbing their hands in glee and saying, "Boy, did we ever put it over on those Dutchmen."

Within the New Democratic Party there were mixed feelings in regard to the complex. I attacked the program on the basis that it appeared to be almost totally financed with public money. If the project failed the public would lose money. If however, the project succeeded, the developers would bang their chests and say, "Look ma, we're captains of industry."

During the 1969 election, Ed Schreyer took no position on the project. He tended to view it favourably since it involved considerable industrial development in the Province but he was not wedded to the principle that, when public money is spent, the public should own the project.

When the NDP assumed power, Schreyer, who was the minister to whom the Manitoba Development Corporation reported, immediately became involved in dealing with the principals of Technopulp. I expressed concern because they did not appear to have any equity in the development. The officials however assured Schreyer that they would confirm an investment of 20 per cent of the total capital cost to substantiate their equity.

After a public announcement confirming the investors' equity, Schreyer felt that any problems associated with the project had been resolved. However when the ultimate figures were revealed, the 20 per cent equity proved to be a sham.

The claim had been based on the building of homes at The Pas. The investors had simply listed the amount being spent on those homes as part of their investment. However the homes were almost totally publicly financed, which meant the investors had no real equity in the project. Furthermore the amount being advanced to them was probably more than the capital cost of the project. In other words, the investors were obtaining a considerable amount of money as profit, simply for undertaking the development.

Several cabinet ministers had misgivings about the program but it was finally decided that since the development was already underway the government had a contractual commitment. There was no alternative but to continue.

Those concerned about the deal maintained that it had not been initiated or sponsored by the NDP but was merely a fulfillment of a commitment made by the previous government Accordingly they insisted those involved with the program, particularly government solicitor Walter Newman, continue to be associated with the program to ensure no suggestion that the government in any way interfered with its development.

The Conservatives suggested that the government, with its socialist bent, wanted to expropriate the project and this suggestion had to be avoided. But it was not necessary to expropriate the project. The government had a debenture which gave what it believed to be was a first charge against all of the Corporations assets. Given the nature of the development it was almost inevitable that the developers would be seeking more financing. When that occurred, there would be tough negotiations about what the Government's participation would be.

The development continued and ultimately, in the summer of 1970, Alexander Kasser, the prime mover and effective owner of the project, asked for an appointment with me since I was the Mines and Resources Minister.

We met in my office on the third floor of the Legislative Building. Kasser proved to be charming and intelligent. He flattered me as being one of the people in cabinet who understood commercial ventures and had an understanding of the transaction itself.

The meeting was more a get-acquainted session than anything of great consequence but there was no doubt that Kasser was a formidable character. A former citizen of Hungary, he told me about his involvement in saving Jews during the Nazi oppression of Hungary during the Second World War.

At the close of the meeting I gained some measure of the depth of Kasser's intelligence. I said, "Mr. Kasser, the government is advancing $90 million to your organization for the construction of this project. Out of this $90 million you are making x millions of dollars. I don't know how much x is and for the moment I am not going to pursue that. Whatever x is, why couldn't we just pay you the x million dollars and, since we are advancing the entire monies to build the project, why could we not own the project and you would obtain the x million as a fee?"

Kasser responded, "Oh, you can't do that."

I asked, "Why not?"

Kasser said,"Because you *didn't* do that."

This was a totally practical and sensible answer. Kasser had no ideological confusion about what was happening. He did not suggest that the public could not operate the project as well as he could. He simply indicated that according to the deal, he would get the fee and also own the project. And there was to be no reneging on the deal. I appreciated the answer. I was convinced that Kasser knew far better what he was doing than did the Roblin administration when it agreed to the financial terms of the project.

Shortly thereafter Len Evans became the minister responsible for the Manitoba Development Corporation. It was his role to monitor the progress of the project. Terrible misgivings were being expressed because large amounts of money were being advanced by the Corporation as its commitment to the project.

An urgent meeting was arranged between MDC director Rex Grose and the cabinet. Following intense questioning, Gross acknowledged that the Corporation was advancing money to the developers on the basis of invoices received for goods yet to be supplied, instead of on the basis of development at the site.

It appeared that Grose, along with Kasser, did not trust the government to keep its commitments. The advancement of funds apparently was devised to make sure that the monies that had been promised would be forthcoming and that no steps would be taken by the government to discontinue funding.

As soon as Grose left the cabinet meeting it was agreed that he should be fired. It was also determined that Evans would engage a consultant to conduct an overview in order to determine what was occurring at The Pas site. For this purpose Evans obtained the services of Stothert Engineering Ltd.

In December 1970 it became apparent that almost the entire $90 million had been advanced to the Kasser group with no indication of when the project would be completed. Desperate cabinet sessions were held to consider the situation. Len Evans and Attorney General Al Mackling urged the government to take over the project. I resisted this position because I was very uncomfortable with the setting of a new direction by someone who was far less acquainted with the project than Kasser.

Nevertheless there was a need to determine whether the project would be completed within the existing framework or the province would be left with a project requiring an undetermined amount of funds in order to be completed.

Schreyer commissioned me to call Kasser in an effort to get an assessment of the situation. That call was one of the more interesting I ever had. It again indicated Kasser's intelligence and ultimate practicality.

I commenced the conversation by asking Kasser how much more money would be required before the project was completed. Kasser responded by saying, "It's finished."

Pursuing the matter I said I was not asking whether it was substantially completed but simply how many more dollars would the government be required to pay to Kasser to get the wheels turning. Kasser responded, "About a million and a half dollars."

I said, "This is what I am concerned with. I'm interested in getting this project completed for the least amount of money possible. There are people here who do not want you on the job because they feel that you are a crook. I don't know whether you are a crook or not. What I also don't know is whether or not the next person will be a crook."

Kasser responded, "The next person may be worse than a crook. He may be an incompetent." In a biography of Talleyrand written by Jean Orieux, Talleyrand is quoted as saying, in regard to a particular matter of which he was aware, "It was worse than a crime. It was a mistake."

Kasser's incisive assessment of the situation made a great impression on me. I admired Kasser both as an individual and for his competence. I was also certain that Kasser would get the job done. I **felt** that Kasser would need more money and the government would be able to negotiate a substantial if not majority, equity position when that occurred.

The government needed an operating project and I was one of the few ministers who wanted to retain Kasser until the project was put into operation. My views, however, did not prevail and the cabinet decided to exercise its right under its debenture and appoint a receiver, thus gaining control of the complex.

The cabinet considered the conventional method of hiring a firm of chartered accountants as professional receivers. I argued that, since it was a private receivership and did not require court appointment, the Province could simply take a top-level lawyer in the Attorney-General's department and appoint him as receiver. This would avoid the burden of paying individuals on a regular percentage basis for being available. With a civil servant as the receiver, his existing salary would continue with his responsibilities devoted to the receivership.

My suggestion was adopted and Liefur Hallgrimson, a senior attorney in the Attorney-General's department, was named as the receiver. The announcement with respect to the takeover of what was now called Churchill Forest Industries was handled with style by the Premier. He appeared one evening on television and, in the best 'cloak and dagger' fashion, announced that the RCMP and other officials had taken possession of the complex – almost at the same time that these officials appeared at the complex in The Pas.

The receivership was accomplished with great efficiency. On January 8, 1971, the Province of Manitoba exercised its right under the debenture to take possession of all of the assets of the Churchill Forest Industries complex. Spofford Engineering was appointed to supervise the continuance of the project and most of the employees remained.

Kasser, knowing that he would be pursued by the Manitoba government, spent the next several years of his life dodging legal proceedings. I suggested that attorney Scott Wright (now a Queen's Bench judge) be engaged to do the legal work in regard to the receivership with the assistance of Charles Huband (now a Court of Appeal judge). My advice was heeded as the two were hired to take all legal proceedings that were incidental to the takeover.

At the same time the government appointed a Commission of Inquiry to review all activities associated with the project, including the activities of the NDP government. Such action was necessary to dispel any suggestion that the government was expropriating a legitimate private entrepreneur for ideological reasons. The Commission of Inquiry included the former Chief Justice of the Court of Appeal C. Rhodes Smith, Leon Mitchell, and Professor Murray Donnelly of the University of Manitoba. The solicitor was D'Arcy McCaffrey, now deceased, who became a prominent civil litigation lawyer in the province.

As expected, when Spofford took over the project, further demands for funds were made. This is inevitable when a new contractor takes over another person's work. The second contractor always has more latitude because he is absolved of any problems that arose during his predecessor's tenure. This is exactly what happened at the forestry complex.

Before Churchill Forest Industries began to operate, many million dollars were advanced. This was done under the supervision of the receiver and Spofford Engineering.

After several months of preparation, the Commission of Inquiry conducted hearings where Schreyer and I gave evidence. Following my presentation, I was cross-examined by Frank Mieghan, the solicitor for the Conservative party.

Mieghan attempted to establish that I was a socialist who wanted ownership of the project for ideological reasons. He asked questions intended to show that I considered the project as my own project. I said when the public advanced 100 per cent of the funds to build the complex, there was no question that the public should own it. However I indicated that while I did not favour the receivership, it was a decision by cabinet, of which I was a member.

Subsequently I was appointed as minister to whom the Churchill Forest Industries complex reported, along with responsibility for the Manitoba Development Corporation.

During that period, I received letters from Kasser, containing information which Kasser felt would improve the development of the project. I passed these letters on to Hallgrimson without comment. It is plain that Kasser believed me to be a kindred spirit. I did have some regard for Kasser even though I abided by the government's decision with respect to the takeover and the pursuing of Kasser by all available civil and criminal means.

After pursuing Kasser for many years Manitoba ultimately made a financial statement which resulted in some funds being returned to the Province but not nearly the amount claimed.

The project continued to experience losses and Kasser continued to criticize its manner of operation. After all civil and criminal proceedings were dropped he provided an interesting footnote to the story. In a public letter to Hallgrimson he noted that Hallgrimson was a lawyer and he was an engineer. But for the last several years Hallgrimson had been required to perform Kasser's job as an engineer and Kasser, through no choice on his part, was required to do Hallgrimson's job – act as a lawyer to defend himself. In Kasser's view he had done a better job performing Hallgrimson's job than Hallgrimson had in performing his job.

The Pas Forestry complex remains an important industry in Manitoba. The Province has written off many millions of dollars and the complex has been transferred to private ownership.

As a private enterprise it has received considerable subsidies in the form of provincial write-offs. It is by no means clear that the private firm is doing a better job in operating the project than when it was owned by the public. What is clear is that Gary Filmon's free enterprise government was uncomfortable with a public operation and was much happier to make all kinds of concessions to the private firm.

Green discusses election strategies with federal NDP leader Tommy Douglas.

Green was one of *Winnipeg Free Press* cartoonist Peter Kuch's favourite targets.

MANITOBA DEVELOPMENT CORPORATION

The Roblin administration, like most other provincial governments in Canada, was wed to the principle of free enterprise.

According to this principle, providing a favourable climate for business was the best method of improving economic conditions. Unfortunately merely adopting a hands-off and laissez-faire attitude did not work. Periods of unemployment and lack of economic growth demanded public involvement. Therefore the Conservative government decided to create a public fund to stimulate private business that could not take the initiative on its own because of problems associated with industrial growth. The government's willingness to put crutches under what was conceded to be an ineffective system was an admission of the failure of free enterprise.

The Manitoba Development Corporation was ostensibly operated by an independent board with capital funds provided by the provincial government. The public only knew the bottom line – the amount of funds transferred to the Corporation. No information was available about how these funds were being distributed, to whom and on what terms.

When Saul Cherniack learned that the Corporation was taking a debenture for some $90 million for the conglomerate developing the forestry complex in The Pas, numerous questions arose about how these funds were being used. The government steadfastly refused to answer.

Indeed Industry and Commerce Minister Gurney Evans said it would be a disaster for any industry if the public knew it was obtaining financial support from the government. The logic of this explanation escaped me. If creditors were aware that the government was advancing money to an industry, I argued, it would make it easier for the company to obtain funds.

One of the last things a government wanted to see was the industry which it was financing becoming insolvent. As a result there was a tendency to provide additional loans to any publicly-financed company in difficulty. This was a basic flaw in the concept.

When the New Democrats came to power they immediately required the Manitoba Development Corporation report to a standing committee of the Legislature. All funds being advanced and all industries receiving money were to be made public. This practice was continued throughout the Schreyer administration.

As a result of this practice, the chairman of the MDC appeared before the committee on a yearly basis. Each loan and other funds advanced were subjected to scrutiny. This scrutiny revealed the extent to which the Roblin administration had engaged in the practice of state-financed capitalism. It also revealed loans and other advances made by the NDP government.

It should be noted that Manitoba was not unique. Almost every province uses public funds to bolster the private sector and success and failure rates were comparable to those experienced by the Manitoba government.

When the New Democrats assumed power, Finance Minister Saul Cherniack should have been the minister to whom the Manitoba Development Corporation reported. Cherniack, however, did not wish to assume this responsibility. As a result the task was initially undertaken by Premier Schreyer and then was shifted to Len Evans, the Minister of Mines, who was a professor in economics.

Evans, who considered himself a true socialist, used the MDC in such a way as to advance some of his political ideas. Notably he considered it a success to attract to the province an aircraft industry which would be almost fully publicly owned. He also financed a Canadian publishing firm which was entirely a product of his economic nationalism.

The Corporation was responsible for some of the major financial controversies which prevailed during the Schreyer administration's term in office. It is fair to say that most of the financial commitments by the Corporation in terms of dollars were made by the Roblin administration. The greatest of these was the Churchill Forest Industry Complex. Other improvident transactions such as Sprague Forest Products also occurred during the Roblin years under a cloak of secrecy.

Major projects undertaken by the Schreyer administration included Flyer Coach Industries, Saunders Aircraft and Masawa Homes. Another financial commitment involved Versatile Manufacturing Ltd.

Versatile was one of the most important manufacturing industries in Manitoba. It was regarded as a financial jewel. However during the first years of the NDP administration, it ran into financial difficulties. In an act of desperation it was forced to seek government assistance.

After examining the program through the Manitoba Development Corporation, the government agreed to make a loan commitment, on the understanding that it would be entitled to hold shares in proportion to the level of funding advanced as against the funding previously advanced by private investors.

The government hired Izzy Asper, a Winnipeg lawyer, to handle the arrangement. The transaction was concluded but Versatile never drew on the funds. Instead it succeeded in arranging private financing on the strength of the government's commitment and overcame its financial difficulties.

As a result the government never became a shareholder in Versatile. However the state capitalism as practised by the Corporation was successful in maintaining and sustaining one of the most important industrial complexes in the province.

Other Corporation endeavors had less happy endings. Indeed after several years it was apparent that its activities were getting out of hand and becoming a potential source of embarrassment. Therefore Schreyer decided to transfer the responsibility for the Corporation from Evans to me. The premier said my experience in law and the business world, as well as my ability to debate and defend the Corporation in the House, were required.

I immediately strengthened the board of the Corporation by appointing businessmen and lawyers. They included Stewart Martin, Maurice Arpin, Jim Hanson, a former manager of the Bank of Canada, and Norman Coghlin, a former president of the Winnipeg Chamber of Commerce.

I said the Board would have total control over its activities except when, as a matter of public policy, the government desired it to take certain action. In such cases I promised to take total responsibility for the government's action and absolve the Board of any responsibility or blame.

I then prepared guidelines which essentially restricted the Board to making financially sound loans and refraining from any financial involvement with industries which would merely compete with an existing Manitoba industry.

This was the first set of guidelines ever received by the Board. It was approved. When Opposition Leader Sidney Spivak learned of the guidelines, he angrily suggested that the government was interfering with the independence of the Manitoba Development Corporation Board. When I denied that charge Spivak, demanded to see the guidelines. I eagerly revealed them knowing they were highly self-serving.

There are great arguments with respect to the government's activities in regard to the Manitoba Development Corporation. Admittedly considerable investment funds were lost in some operations. There is also no doubt, considerable expertise was obtained in the commercial world and some of the industries funded did operate on a relatively sound basis. Two companies, Dormond Industries and Dawn Plastics, for which the government was fully responsible, did struggle through.

The major problem associated with public involvement in commercial enterprises was the amount of criticism with respect to the use of public funds, in contrast to those totally funded by private sources.

The issue is not completely philosophical. Every government has found it necessary to use public funds to stimulate and finance private industry. It is still being done on a scale which would dwarf the amounts advanced by the government of Manitoba through the Manitoba Development Corporation.

Gary Filmon's Conservative government continued to use public funds to finance private industries, but did so on an ad-hoc basis with no public exposure of the recipient's operations.

For practical, rather than philosophical purposes, public investment in private industry is a fact in Canada. The Schreyer government attempted with less success than failure to have funds advanced on a sound financial basis. However the positive impact on several industries in the province justify the use of such a policy. The investment in McCain Foods, for instance, was sensible on a commercial basis and also made sense with regard to establishment of a food-processing industry in Manitoba.

I believe the public should be a necessary participant in public industrial and commercial development. The basis of its participation is the matter which is subject to argument.

The guidelines produced did not result in any significant losses to the government of Manitoba.

Another aspect of government involvement in commercial and industrial enterprises is labour. The labour unions in Manitoba were closely allied with the NDP government.

As a result, in the cases of Saunders Aircraft and Flyer Industries, they believed they should obtain special benefits for their members by virtue of this alignment. As a matter of fact the lawyer for Canadian Auto Workers and one of its main officials came to Winnipeg to discuss a severance plan for employees of Saunders Aircraft when the company was being dismantled.

Bitterly they learned there would be nothing more than what would occur in normal private sector operations. They indicated an intention to grieve the matter and their lawyer warned he would finance the case all the way to the Supreme Court of Canada. However the company was closed down and no further union activity took place.

Insofar as Flyer Industries Ltd. was concerned, the employees went on strike during a by-election, believing the strike would have some political impact. To the disappointment, surprise and chagrin of the labour movement, the government gave no special aid to the employees.

A side story to this strike came one morning when I was awakened at my Westgate residence by my eight-year-old daughter Cathy. "Daddy, there are men with signs standing outside the house," she said. I looked out the window and saw Flyer picketers in front of the residence. I said, "Cathy, those men have a right to be there. Not only do they have a right to be there, but your Daddy fought for their right to be there."

The picketers were offered coffee and I went to work through the picket line. Within hours the picketers disappeared, never to return.

SAUNDERS AIRCRAFT

The story of Saunders Aircraft deserves some mention. Saunders was a small eastern aircraft firm that was financially strapped. Len Evans claimed success in luring the company to Manitoba. The bait was the Manitoba Development Corporation's willingness to provide the $1.5 million to get the company on its feet.

However that $1.5 million gradually turned into a financial hemorrhage. Many millions more were advanced to Saunders, which still had not obtained a certificate of air-worthiness from the federal government. The provincial government continued to request the Manitoba Development Corporation Board to advance more funds until the amount reached $30 million.

In actual fact that amount was not outrageous for the development of an aircraft manufacturing company, which was providing over 200 paying jobs in the Gimli area. However the difference between original prospects and ultimate requirements was too much to endure and ultimately the government was required to bail out.

A letter was prepared to the MDC and released to the press on a Friday afternoon. Significantly a by-election was pending in Wolseley constituency, where Murdoch MacKay was the NDP candidate. No doubt it would have been preferable for the government and MacKay if the announcement been made after the by-election but that was not to be. Sid Parsons, chairman of the Manitoba Development Corporation was willing to delay the announcement, but I believed it was far more politically damaging for the government to delay an announcement cutting off funds in order to facilitate an election campaign.

The Saturday newspapers headlined the Saunders story, indicating wrongly that *all* funds had been cut off. This necessitated a press conference on Monday in order to ensure those who had prior commitments that the

Corporation intended to honour those commitments while seeking a purchaser for the company. The continued operation of Saunders made it more saleable.

I had phoned MacKay on Friday night and advised him of the announcement. While MacKay was startled, he accepted the explanation with the same class exhibited throughout his political life. On the following Tuesday the by-election was held and MacKay was narrowly defeated by Conservative Bob Wilson.

The Saunders assets were subsequently sold on a fire-sale basis and produced very little return. The ultimate loss to the public of Manitoba amounted to some $30 million.

FLYER COACH INDUSTRIES/MISAWA HOMES

Flyer Coach Industries has a different scenario than most Manitoba Development Corporation investments. The company had been operating in Manitoba for some years prior to the election of the NDP government and from time to time had sought and received some public financing.

During the first years of the Schreyer administration, Flyer approached the Corporation for assistance. It was agreed that monies would be advanced on the understanding that the public would become a shareholder in proportion to the risk in making the investment. Ultimately the public became virtually the sole owner of Flyer.

The future of Flyer Coach seemed much brighter than that of Saunders Aircraft. Although funding was continually advanced, it was on a much lower scale and resulted in Winnipeg becoming the major manufacturer of trolley buses in North America. It continued to function partly because of the state capitalism practised by the Manitoba Development Corporation.

In regard to Flyer, I received a rude awakening in terms of public involvement in commercial enterprises. Normally, members of the Legislature praised local industry. Rarely did one hear them question the viability or the performance of a local industry which was important to the province. Indeed until a local private enterprise actually became insolvent, no public spokesman questioned its performance.

When the public is involved, however, the situation is quite different, as indicated by the constant criticism of any government involvement through the Manitoba Development Corporation. For instance, Opposition MLAs questioned whether Saunders Aircraft was even eligible to obtain an aircraft worthiness certificate. As for Flyer the question periods during the Schreyer administration's second term often focussed on the viability of that firm.

In this regard, the strangest example of such public questioning took place in connection with an order for buses which Flyer Industries had obtained from the city of San Francisco. In order to bid on the tender, a $28 million performance bond was required. The Canadian Indemnity Company, represented by Harley Vannon, an outspoken critic of the government during the Autopac debate, was prepared to grant the bond, provided the province accepted 25 per-cent ($7 million) responsibility. The government agreed.

Partway through the contract there were some difficulties at the plant and Vannon, apparently for political reasons, publicly questioned whether Flyer Industries was capable of fulfilling the contract of which his company had guaranteed $21 million. Perhaps Vannon believed the government would ensure the contract was met regardless of the expense to the Manitoba Development Corporation. He was quickly made aware that such action would not occur.

At a meeting of the MDC's committee responsible for Flyer, I told Corporation chairman Sid Parsons to get in touch with Vannon and advise him that the minister was well aware the public would lose $7 million if the contract was not fulfilled. I also instructed Parsons to indicate that, while I was unhappy with this situation, I was quite prepared to announce in the Legislature that the government was **ready** to forfeit its $7 million because Flyer Industries could not fulfill the contract. I also told Parsons that if Vannon questioned whether I had the courage to make such an announcement, he should ask those who knew me to see if, indeed, the announcement would be made.

Emphasizing that I was prepared to make that announcement, I requested Parsons to ask Vannon whether he was equally willing to announce to his shareholders the loss of $21 million.

My message was passed on and had the desired effect. Nothing further was heard from Vannon with respect to the capability of Flyer to perform the contract. The company did fulfill the contract and no funds were forfeited. Flyer continues to be an important bus manufacturer in North America.

The situation with respect to Misawa Homes deserves some mention. Misawa is a Japanese house firm which manufactures houses in Japan on a scale which is comparable to McDonalds manufacturing hamburgers.

When the Manitoba Development Corporation was under the supervision of Len Evans, it made an arrangement with Misawa to invest $2 million on a 50/50 basis to develop a unique home building industry in Manitoba.

Misawa did manufacture homes in Manitoba. Many were sold and can be seen at the present time. However it became apparent to me that continued advancement of funds to Misawa would not result in any profitable returns to either investor.

MDC chairman, Sid Parsons, several other members of the corporation's board and I went to Japan in order to indicate to Misawa that further investment would not be profitable.

When I met with company officials, I experienced a business climate which was different than anything I had known. The Misawa people were not prepared to concede defeat. They wished to continue making investments on the basis that the province would honour its commitment to invest 50 per-cent.

That investment was not commercially profitable but it did not result in a substantial net loss to the province. Therefore the government reluctantly continued the investment until Misawa gracefully wound up the company.

NELSON RIVER DEVELOPMENT

One of the major thrusts of the Roblin administration was the development of the hydro-electric power generated by the waters of Nelson River.

This development had several obvious advantages. It constituted a renewable resource which could be harnessed to produce inexpensive energy domestically. As well, it could serve as an incentive for industry to locate in Manitoba.

It had the additional advantage of making excess electric power available for sale to other provinces and the United States.

The hydro-electric power development proceeded without any serious criticism until it reached a phase scheduled for the late 1960s. That phase involved the construction of a dam to facilitate diversion of water from the Churchill River to the Nelson River at a location known as South Indian Lake.

South Indian Lake was similar to other remote settlements in the province. Its population consisted largely of native people but there was no established Indian reserve. Instead it was populated by those who had left other reserves and built a settlement at that location.

I first learned about this project when I interviewed Dr. Cass Booy and Dr. Robert Newbury, professors at the University of Manitoba, as part of research with respect to my new responsibility as critic of natural resources. Harry Enns was the minister of this portfolio.

Booie and Newbury indicated that raising the water levels at South Indian Lake would result in forcing a viable Indian community with relatively few problems to move to another location. This revelation came as somewhat of a surprise to me since little had been said in the Legislature about this impact. The matter was raised in the Legislature by Liberal Gordon Johnston. I took over from then on.

Quickly becoming the Opposition spokesman on this topic, I raised the matter on numerous occasions, offering attacks on the government's lack of knowledge of the problem and its apparent lack of concern about the relocation of the Indian population.

(During the same session I introduced a private member's resolution calling for the removal of a restriction on the eligibility of Aboriginal people to seek election to school boards. Subsequently Education Minister Donald Craik brought in legislation to rectify the problem and credited me for raising a valid point. As a result I became known as a spokesman on native issues.)

Meanwhile concern about the flooding of South Indian Lake gained momentum in the Legislature. The government did not appear to have given the issue proper attention and many accepted it as an established fact that the flooding would take place. Construction commenced before a licence authorizing the water diversion was granted.

When Enns finally scheduled public hearings on the matter large audiences attended. Residents of South Indian Lake were represented by legal counsel. During the hearings it became apparent that the government had not conducted proper environmental studies or determined the benefits and costs associated with the project. In particular, the costs of relocating the Indian band and subsequent social problems were not considered.

The matter came to a head when Saul Cherniack obtained leaked information about a report prepared at the Government's request. Written by Hedland Menzies, it was entitled "Transition in the North" and presumably dealt with the issue. When Cherniack demanded the release of this report in the legislature, the government refused maintaining that it was confidential. But when Hydro officials finally appeared before a legislative committee, the entire issue of the flooding of South Indian Lake and its consequences, as well as the Government's unpreparedness, was revealed.

As previously indicated, Premier Walter Weir called an election in the midst of these committee meetings. The fiasco created by Conservative ineptitude in dealing with the South Indian Lake development became an issue in the campaign.

Various university professors, including Booie and Newbury prevailed upon the NDP to give a public undertaking that the lake would not be flooded. Since I was intimately acquainted with the issue I urged Schreyer not to give such a commitment. None was given. Instead, while I dealt with the issue at every public meeting during the election, I was very careful to avoid any commitment to refrain from raising water levels at South Indian Lake. Schreyer, who knew little about the program because he had not been in the province when the issue arose, followed my lead.

As a result the NDP merely promised to review whether the flooding of the lake was essential to the continued development of the Nelson River.

Only Liberal leader Bobby Bend made an irresponsible commitment. In mid-campaign he promised South Indian Lake would not be flooded if his party came to power. As indicated by the results, that commitment did not gain the Liberals any electoral points.

When the New Democrats won the election, they inherited the South Indian Lake controversy. Schreyer was rather doubtful about altering the program because the Nelson River development seemed to be desirable. However many cabinet ministers who had been more involved in the project in the past expressed concerns. As a result Schreyer agreed to review the decision with respect to the high-level diversion of South Indian Lake.

In order to conduct this review the government hired David Cass-Beggs, a former chairman of the Saskatchewan Hydro-Electric Commission and a distinguished figure in the field of hydro-electric development. Senior officials of Manitoba Hydro generally favorably the choice because of his stature, experience and credibility.

As Minister of Mines and Natural Resources, Len Evans had a pivotal role in dealing with hydro development because his department would be granting the water licences. I recommended the appointment of Booy and Newbury to the Manitoba Water Commission and encouraged the hiring of Cass-Beggs. A committee of Cabinet made the ultimate decision.

The review came to the conclusion, supported by senior Hydro officials, that low-level diversion, which would reduce the level of flooding from 32 feet to 16 feet, would be equally as economical as a high-level diversion. It also called for regulation of Lake Winnipeg which would result in storage of water in the lake during the summer and release of water during the winter season when hydro-electric power was required.

This approach, which had long been considered by Manitoba Hydro, ensured the same level of power which would result from high-level flooding but would not require relocation of the South Indian Lake community.

The government accepted the report. High-level flooding of the lake would be reduced, with no relocation of the community, while Lake Winnipeg regulation would supplement the needs resulting from the reduced flood level.

But which step would be implemented first? Since the study, along with information supplied to Cabinet, indicated very little financial difference, the government decided to proceed first with regulation Lake Winnipeg. This would provide more time to measure the effects of the Churchill River diversion on South Indian Lake and deal with any dislocation and resource problems.

That decision prompted much debate. Opposition Leader Sidney Spivak repeatedly accused the government of adopting a political program which would cost many millions of dollars. He suggested this program had been adopted in order to save embarrassment to those who had criticized the high-level diversion. The Conservatives believed the sequence was wrong and the low-level diversion should be the first phase in the new development.

The controversy resulted in a series of meetings held by the Water Commission in the communities affected. Those meetings caused me considerable discomfort.

Members of the Commission, which was represented by its own counsel, Dale Gibson, wanted to conduct hearings rather than meetings. I was then Minister of Natural Resources and insisted that I would only appoint the Commission to conduct informational meetings because hearings involved a legal status that could be the subject of judicial review. In my view, this would leave the impression that the ultimate decision could be altered. But that decision had already been made.

Newbury and Booy sent a written message to me, indicating that they would hold hearings which would not have full legal effect. I refused to participate in this type of facade. I said the Commission was being requested to hold meetings, not hearings, and that would be their mandate.

That response prompted the resignation of Newbury from the Commission. Documentation with respect to the resignation indicated that the government's position with respect to the purpose of the meetings was on a much firmer and legitimate basis than the Commission's proposal.

I had no difficulty in defending my position before the Manitoba Legislature, insisting the Commission's proposal was an apparent subterfuge.

At the Commission meetings in various communities proceeded, Cass-Beggs and I explained the government's program. A meeting at Norway House attracted considerable attention because of the presence of former premier D.L. Campbell, who was a member of the Manitoba Hydro Commission Board.

His presence was initiated at a previous meeting of the Public Utilities Committee. That meeting was marked by a split between Kris Christianson, a Manitoba Hydro official, and Cass-Beggs, who was committee chairman. Christianson made a public protest against the Lake Winnipeg regulation decision. At one point Cass-Beggs had said, "Everyone knows that there will be both higher and lower water levels in Lake Winnipeg than were reached historically."

Challenging the statement at Norway House Campbell said, "Mr. Cass-Beggs says that everyone knows that the lowest and highest levels of Lake

Winnipeg have not yet been reached. How does he substantiate this statement? I don't know it." Cass-Beggs responded, "When I said that everyone knows, I concede that I did not take into account that Campbell did not know it."

The criticism came from both sides. Some did not believe regulation of Lake Winnipeg did enough to protect erosion problems. Others demanded no flooding whatsoever at South Indian Lake. Meanwhile regulation of the Lake proceeded and before the 1973 election, it was virtually in operation.

After the election, developments occurred in regard to South Indian Lake flooding which were to have profound effects. Studies of the project had determined that the diversion of Nelson River waters would flood some reservation land belonging to the Nelson House Band. That land was not inhabited and the Band could be easily compensated with equivalent lands in the vicinity. It seemed to be a minor problem.

However members of the Nelson River Band saw the matter quite differently. They saw the possible encroachment of water on Indian reserve land as a bargaining weapon with which to extract funds and other concessions from the Province.

The Northern Flood Committee was formed. Including all communities in the vicinity of the Nelson River development, its objective was to obtain compensation for any and all impacts of the development on their communities.

The Committee made representations to the federal government which, although a partner to the Nelson River development, agreed to finance the group and support it in compensation claims. This was an irresponsible action because the federal government had the power and should simply have exchanged the affected lands for other acceptable land in the area.

In discussions with the Northern Flood Committee, the Manitoba government indicated that, even though it was not legally required, it was willing to pay compensation to all communities and individuals who could demonstrate damage by the Nelson River development. However the committee was represented by Winnipeg solicitors who would not agree to such a settlement. They were supported by Warren Allemand, the federal minister of Indian Affairs.

Manitoba insisted that the problem could be easily resolved since the federal government was a signatory to the agreement which authorized the project. Ottawa need only expropriate the portion of land that would be affected by the development and replace it with lands made available by the Province. Because this was unacceptable to the reserve, Ottawa refused to act.

Protracted negotiations ensued with no agreement. The federal government threatened to support the Band in obtaining an injunction against the

South Indian Lake diversion. At a meeting attended by Allemand and the solicitor for the Northern Flood Committee, the subject of the injunction arose. I responded to this intimidation by saying, "Go and get your god-dammed injunction."

The following day an article in the *Winnipeg Tribune*, correctly quoted my comments. I approached reporter Jenny Bowman and said, "I didn't know you had taken to listening at keyholes." She answered, "We didn't have to listen at any keyhole. You could be heard all over the building."

In any event no injunction was sought. Instead the federal and provincial governments agreed to appoint Leon Mitchell to mediate a settlement. Finally a draft agreement was proposed. It seemed to be acceptable to the province government and the Northern Flood Committee. But I immediately realized that the province could not settle.

According to the agreement, if an arbitrator believed or made a finding that damages had occurred to any of the communities or individuals, he could make an order requiring the province to implement a program as compensation for those damages. In effect, the arbitrator would have the authority to direct the province to implement policy in northern Manitoba for the communities concerned. This was totally unacceptable to me and I advised the Premier accordingly.

Some Hydro officials and solicitors believed those arguments were unfounded because, under the agreement, no arbitrator could do more than give compensation to the communities affected. That compensation had to be commensurate with the damage suffered.

I agreed with the need for compensation but argued it should be determined by a court. This agreement did not provide that avenue. My detractors disagreed, insisting the agreement would be interpreted in the proper fashion.

At a Manitoba Development Corporation policy seminar at Falcon Lake in 1977, I thought of a solution. If the agreement could be interpreted as providing compensation only to the amount of damages incurred, why not insert a clause saying so? Lying in bed, I devised a clause, but having no pen I went to Murdoch MacKay's room at 2:00 a.m. and knocked on his door. When a bleary eyed MacKay answered the door I asked, "Do you have a pencil?" The astonished MacKay found a pencil. The two of us then went to the sauna where I explained my intentions and wrote out the clause which I thought should be added to the agreement. The clause read:

> "Notwithstanding anything hereinbefore contained, bearing or
> capable of bearing any different and/or contrary interpretation, it is
> expressly understood and agreed by all the parties hereto, that in
> any adjudication arising hereunder, before the arbitrator or other-

wise whereby damages may be awarded, the amount of such damage shall be limited in quantum, to such amount as would compen-
sate the person or persons making a claim for such adverse affect
suffered by them that are directly attributable to the project."

I immediately conveyed the clause to Schreyer and, after some discussion,
it was added to the draft agreement which had been presented to the
provincial authorities. It was signed by those authorities, including the
Premier, and sent to Ottawa.

Ottawa refused to sign the added stipulation even though it was exactly
what the negotiators had claimed should occur. Once more there was an
impasse.

The issue remained in limbo and ultimately became a significant part of
the 1977 provincial election campaign. The Reserve, the Northern Flood
Committee and the federal government claimed an agreement had been
negotiated which the province had refused to sign. Indeed an agreement had
been discussed but the Manitoba government wanted a provision to ensure
that those affected by the Nelson River development program would be
entitled to compensation which would not exceed what would be awarded by
a court if there had been a legal entitlement decision.

The federal government and the Flood Committee had refused to accept
such a stipulation and the agreement remained unsigned. During the election
campaign, Liberal Leader Charles Huband strongly criticized the province for
failing to sign the agreement while the Conservatives tried to exploit the
disagreement between the government and the Flood Committee.

As indicated, the government's refusal to sign the Northern Flood
Agreement figured prominently in the 1977 election and many thought the
New Democrats would suffer as a result. The party did lose the election, but it
won every seat which contained the Indian communities that formed the
Northern Flood group.

Following the election, my last act as a minister was to send a letter to
incoming Premier Sterling Lyon. I wrote that signing the Northern Flood
Agreement would be an abdication of government responsibility for the social
and economic development of the citizens of northern Manitoba. I felt it
would be totally wrong for the Conservative government to sign. I indicated
I would support the government if it did not sign.

At the opening day of the first legislative session after the election, the
Conservatives, contrary to all precedents, permitted a question period. I rose
and asked whether the new administration intended to sign the Agreement. I
got an equivocal answer. Subsequently the new government signed the

Northern Flood Agreement with no substantive changes. As a result countless claims were made under the Agreement. Ironically I served as counsel for the Norway House First Nation which had successfully pursued a claim.

In 1995 the federal government, the Manitoba government and Manitoba Hydro were engaged in extensive negotiations in an attempt to extricate themselves from the obligations under the Agreement through payments to the reserves concerned. The amount could reach the billion-dollar figure.

It should be noted that both provincial and federal bureaucrats frequently referred to the outrageousness of the agreement's requirements and recalled that my vigorous opposition had prevented the NDP government from executing it.

PART FIVE

THE DEMISE

THE BEGINNING OF THE END

Immediately following the 1977 election loss to the Conservatives, I re-established my legal practice by resuming work as a litigation lawyer. Although I would have been welcomed in various Winnipeg law firms, I preferred to practise on my own.

I set up an office which was ideally suited to the type of work I intended to do. Approaching several lawyer friends, I proposed that when their files bogged down to such a degree they couldn't look at them, they should hand those files to me and I would resolve them. This strategy was successful.

As I became more active in the field of civil litigation, my practice flourished. By all standards I was one of the most active litigation lawyers in the Court of Queen's Bench and the Court of Appeal.

On the political front, the New Democratic Party prepared to be in opposition. Among the new members was Jay Cowan, a former party organizer, who, in 1977 had been sent to the Churchill constituency to search for a candidate. Ed Schreyer had lured a prominent Churchill resident to run for the nomination but Cowan had ideas of his own. He organized the constituency and captured the nomination.

Since Cowan was not yet a Canadian citizen, having left the U.S. during the Vietnam war, many accused him of being a draft dodger. But, as far as the party was concerned, that was irrelevant. In any event he won the Churchill nomination and was elected. His entry into the NDP caucus was an important event insofar as I was concerned. Cowan was part of the party administration which opposed wage and price controls. He was also aligned with the women militants, which meant he was a strong opponent of mine.

With many veterans, the New Democratic Party in opposition was formidable. Schreyer placed me to his immediate right in the Legislative chamber, an honoured location indicating the occupant's experience and importance. The current senior New Democrat, Saul Cherniack, had left cabinet during the last session and chose to sit in the back row, presumably as a demonstration of his disdain for prestige and status. His move proved to be short-lived.

When the legislature met it was apparent that Schreyer had no taste for leading the opposition and discussion about leadership reached a fever level. Once more I and some fellow MLAs, were mentioned as potential leaders. But the anti-Green forces in the administration and enemies within the caucus were desperate to prevent my accession.

In particular Cherniack, urged on by the feminists, who now considered him a friend, asked Schreyer to move him to the front row. Schreyer complied but placed Cherniack to his left, rather than his right. Traditionally the seat to the right of the Opposition leader went to the second in command which made me House leader of the Opposition.

Opponents were obviously unhappy with my status. The matter came to a head in an embarrassing moment when Speaker Harry Graham announced the start of the question period and both Cherniack and I stood up. Schreyer was not in the chamber. With two New Democrats on their feet, the Speaker did not know which one to designate as the deputy leader since there had been no such indication. Who should take precedence, the member for Inkster or the member for St. John's? In a shrewd move Graham called for the deputy leader of the Opposition and both men quickly sat down. Then I rose and was recognized as the member for Inkster.

When I conveyed this information to Schreyer, the leader said that when he was not in the chamber, the House leader would stand for him. While there was still no deputy leader, it meant I would speak for the leader when he was not present.

Soon after the legislature met, speculation about Schreyer's future ended with the announcement that he had been asked by Prime Minister Trudeau to become Governor General of Canada and had accepted. This left the leadership in the New Democratic Party in a state of chaos.

The party administration desperately feared an unsatisfactory outcome if the caucus chose its own leader. It was quite possible I would gain that designation and if that occurred they feared my abilities might ultimately make me the choice for the party leadership. In addition, some within the administration wanted to elevate newly-elected Wilson Parasiuk to the leadership. But this move required time so Parasiuk could demonstrate his ability as a member of the legislature.

As a result three simultaneous operations were underway with respect to replacing Schreyer as leader.

Party president Muriel Smith and the bureaucracy aligned with Saul Miller and Cherniack developed a scenario whereby the provincial council would appoint elder statesman Cherniack as interim leader until a leadership convention could be held.

The suggestion was attractive because Cherniack professed his willingness to accept the position only on a temporary basis. This would facilitate a full-blown leadership campaign, the benefits of which would accrue to the party organization. The administration was also attracted to Cherniack because they feared my support within the party would result in my gaining the leadership – particularly if I was also temporary leader.

On the other hand caucus members believed they had a right to choose their legislative leader. This view was shared by my supporters who felt they could command a majority of caucus in favour of this view.

The third group consisted of Cowan and Ron McBryde, who supported Howard Pawley. They saw Pawley as one who would fit into their future plans for the party which called for a strong alignment between the trade union movement and militant feminists. Initially the Pawley forces were not adverse to Cherniack becoming the temporary leader since they accepted at face value his assurance that he would not seek the leadership. This would provide time to build up their candidate during an extended leadership campaign.

Caucus members Jim Walding, Ben Hanuschak, Bud Boyce and Russell Doern strongly supported me. They had seen enough of the Cherniack and Miller machinations to be completely mistrustful of Cherniack's statement with respect to the temporary nature of his position. They also did not want him used as a stalking horse for party bureaucracy's ultimate choice of Parasiuk.

Doern, Hanuschak and Boyce started canvassing party members. When the Pawley forces realized that the caucus members preferred to choose their own legislative leader, rather than leaving the matter to the Provincial Council, they too began to marshall support for the immediate selection of their candidate. Meanwhile it became apparent that Parasiuk had no caucus support.

At a subsequent caucus meeting, Miller and to a lesser extent, Cherniack, argued vociferously that caucus had no right to name its legislative leader. By doing so, they argued, the caucus would be attempting to exert an unfair influence on the party. The position was ironic since in 1968 Cherniack and Miller had argued successfully that the caucus should issue a statement expressing its opposition to me as leader and support for Schreyer, who was not a candidate.

That argument had no impact this time because the Pawley forces knew their candidate would get ten votes. They did not wish to take a chance on Cherniack becoming the acting leader and then, on the basis of his performance, accepting a draft to run for the official leadership.

So the real contest was between Pawley and myself. I was portrayed by opponents as a tough, vindictive and hard-hitting politician. On the other hand, Pawley was considered a moderate and more reasonable person who could compromise and consult with others.

The caucus gave 10 votes for Pawley, eight for me and three for Cherniack. Brian Corrin, who expressed his disgust with the entire procedure, refused to cast a ballot. This would cost him dearly in the future.

Supporting me were Tom Barrow of Flin Flon, Ben Hanuschak of Burrows, Bud Boyce of Winnipeg Centre, Jim Walding of St. Vital, Peter Fox of Kildonan, Sam Uskiw of Lac du Bonnet and Russ Doern of Elmwood. Ironically those who had been part of the 1968 caucus and whom Cherniack and Miller had insisted could not get along with me, voted for me.

The aftermath of this vote and the fate of my supporters deserves mention. Barrow retired in 1981. Fox, a former speaker and a senior member of the legislature also retired. Doern, a former cabinet minister and party activist for many years, was left out of the Pawley cabinet and eventually resigned from the party to run unsuccessfully as an independent.

Jim Walding was not given a cabinet post in Pawley's administration but was appointed as Speaker. As Speaker he ran afoul of the government because of his rulings in regard to the French language issue. He subsequently resigned from the speakership and, following the 1986 election, sat as a backbencher.

In March 1988 when the legislature was almost equally divided, Walding cast the deciding vote against the Pawley administration on its budgetary measures. This resulted in the defeat of the government and the election of the Conservatives.

Hanuschak, Boyce and I believed we were being driven out of the party as well and ultimately left the NDP and to form the Progressive Party. Uskiw was appointed agriculture minister in the Paulley government but had virtually no power. He maintained that all of his actions had to be approved by the trade union movement. He did not run in the 1986 election, left the New Democratic Party and became an active fund-raiser for the Conservatives.

I did not consider the caucus vote on the leadership to be a defeat. Of the three votes for Cherniack, two were by Miller and Cherniack. The third vote was by Larry Desjardins, who had been very close to me on most issues considered by the cabinet. However for Desjardins the most important issue – which he had championed throughout his political career – was public aid to Roman Catholic private schools. On this question he could never accept me as leader.

After the first vote in the caucus I suggested there be no second ballot and that Pawley be declared the legislative leader. This was a foregone conclusion since Cherniack, Miller and Desjardins would never support me.

The actions taken by the caucus upset NDP officials, but there was no provision in the party's constitution which covered the situation. It was entirely appropriate and in accordance with parliamentary tradition that a caucus choose its leader. What remained to be decided was a leader for the New Democratic Party itself.

Prior to the caucus vote, Uskiw and Pawley came to my home. Pawley wanted to explain his position with respect to the leadership. As a long-time activist in the party, he believed a run for the leadership was a natural step to take, particularly because of his association with the feminist movement and people such as Cowan and McBryde. Pawley said he had no problem with me personally. It was clear to me that Pawley was not opposed to me because of any acrimony, but simply because of my own leadership ambitions.

I indicated that I was not certain about running for the leadership. Such a contest, particularly if it was postponed, could create serious problems for me in re-establishing my law practice. Pawley said he hoped the race would take place at a time when I could be a participant.

Uskiw then explained that since opposing me in 1968 he had felt bad. Therefore he would not do it again and would vote for me, at least on the first ballot.

The meeting ended on friendly terms. I was satisfied that if Pawley became the leader, I would retain in the role I had played under Schreyer's leadership.

When the party council met, those who wanted Cherniack as the interim leader were still quite angry about what had occurred. However, the council adopted the position taken by the caucus and formally named Pawley as the temporary leader of the New Democratic Party.

The only contentious issue was the date of the leadership convention. I argued for an early date, which would give me the option of participating. If it was delayed until the fall, it was almost certain I could not consider running.

But the council, persuaded by the fact that a later convention would involve a series of debates throughout the province which would stimulate interest in the party and increase party membership, voted in favour of a fall convention. That meant I would not be a candidate, but I was not disturbed. In fact, the circumstances which had induced me to be a candidate in 1968 no longer prevailed.

As a result there was no leadership crisis within the party and no need for a catalyst to unseat an incumbent leader. There were also a number of acceptable candidates. I was quite comfortable and felt certain that Pawley would use my experience and abilities in the same way – if not more so – than Schreyer because Pawley lacked the strength of the former Premier.

In making this assessment I failed to take into account the fact that Pawley was so weak, he would be ruled by supporters. Those supporters, particularly Cowan and McBryde and others who would flock to him after the convention, were all opposed to me. They would make it their business to eliminate any influence I had within the party. But that development was yet to come.

The leadership convention was held at the Winnipeg Convention Centre on November 2, 1979. The candidates were Pawley, party president Muriel Smith, and MLA Russell Doern.

Doern ran a spirited campaign but, given the party's attitude towards him, had no chance. He ran a poor third while Smith ran a rather strong second. As expected, Pawley became the new leader of the New Democratic Party on November 4, 1979.

Aside from the leadership contest, one of the main features of the convention was a resolution instigated by the trade union movement. It would have prohibited employers from hiring employees during a legal strike.

Everyone acquainted with the subject knew that I would not support this resolution. In all my years as spokesman for labour causes, I had supported the principle of free collective bargaining, which meant an absence of restrictions on employers and employees. That resolution had been proposed at the previous convention, after the defeat of the NDP, when I was in Britain. It was passed unanimously without debate.

At the 1979 leadership convention I was present and very determined to at least force a debate on the resolution. When it was presented to the floor, I opposed it. I asked the convention to maintain its historical support for the trade union's position, a support based on the free collective bargaining process. I argued that interference by the state in that process would be ultimately counter-productive to the trade union movement. It would also lead to a future government passing a law suggesting that workers who were on strike could not seek other employment, I warned. This would be supported by the trade union movement because it would require all employees to be on strike.

My prediction proved to be true in principle. Recent anti-scab legislation in Canada requires all unionized employees to go on strike and to return to work by either relegating them to walk the picket line or search for other employment.

The resolution was finally approved, but while it had received unanimous support at the previous convention, this time more than one-third of the delegates backed my position and opposed it. Significantly, those standing in opposition on a recorded vote were Cherniack, Desjardins and probably a majority of the legislative caucus.

The caucus, under Pawley's official leadership, began in late 1979. I continued to exercise influence and on most issues, was successful in getting my positions adopted. But my status as a power behind the throne did not sit well with most people who had promoted Pawley's leadership. They resented my past influence in the party and were determined to ensure this situation did not prevail. The vehicle for such action would be the national New Democratic Party scheduled for November 1979 in Ottawa.

COUP D'ETAT

As was our practice, my wife and I attended the 1979 national NDP convention. For a number of years I had been a vice-president and at the 1970 convention received third-highest number of votes ever cast for that position, closely behind Charles Taylor, the most popular member of the party, and David Lewis, whose name was virtually synonymous with the CCF and NDP.

Despite being a vice-president, I had been at odds with the national party establishment for some years. This began when I took a position directly opposite to the one adopted by leader Lewis in the 1972 election. At that time Robert Stanfield led the Conservatives and Pierre Trudeau led the Liberals.

When the results came in on election night the Liberals and Conservatives were virtually tied with the Liberals electing two more members that the Conservatives – not enough to form a majority government. While the public waited anxiously to hear Trudeau's intentions, Stanfield held the first press conference and indicated his party would vote against the Trudeau administration since it had been defeated at the polls.

At a separate press conference Trudeau announced that since no party had achieved a majority he would face Parliament and leave the decision to the MPs. Immediately following Trudeau's statement, Lewis appeared at the same press conference and announced the NDP would seek to obtain its objectives through a minority government which Canadian voters had elected. The NDP would support the "chastened Prime Minister" if reasonable legislation was proposed.

Shortly thereafter, at a meeting of the NDP federal council, Lewis sought support for his position. Several did support him. I did not. I said the NDP was in a position of a tail trying to wag the dog. Not only was it unacceptable it would be unsuccessful. In my view, Lewis had given up a tremendous opportunity. He believed the leader should have waited several days to permit the public to speculate about the NDP position and then held his own separate press conference.

I suggested if that had occurred Lewis could have said that the public of Canada had defeated the Liberal government and the New Democrats would endorse that defeat. As a result, when Parliament was called, no group could command a majority, thus ensuring the defeat of the Trudeau administration and an early election. In that event the contest would have been between the Conservatives and the NDP.

When I stated this position, some people at the meeting seemed to accept its validity. Indeed several took the floor and in a backhanded way complimented me for my strategy. But they suggested it now could not take place. Meanwhile Lewis, who professed continued friendship with me, was hurt by what was said, not so much because of the criticism but probably because he recognized its validity.

In any event as a result of those comments was generally on the outs with the establishment. They tolerated my presence because Manitoba delegates continued to designate me as their vice-president, but indicated in many ways they would be just as happy without my presence.

At the 1979 convention, my Manitoba opponents saw their opportunity. David Orlikow, Wilson Parasiuk, Jay Cowan, Muriel Smith and others organized a group to challenge my position as a national vice-president. This action astonished me. Still enjoying a high level of prestige within the party, I thought my non-participation in the leadership contest would satisfy those who believed I had too much power. The reverse was true. My detractors regarded my absence as evidence of my weakness and irrelevance.

Although vice-presidents of the national party were elected by all delegates, traditionally the Manitoba caucus named its choice. This choice was then placed on a document known as the establishment slate. Those selected by this non-official nominating committee generally were chosen, although it was not unprecedented for someone to divert from the slate.

The Manitoba group scheduled a meeting at a room in the Royal York Hotel, the site of the convention. Approximately 30 delegates attended the meeting. More than twenty had been involved in the pre-arranged decision to oust me. I allowed my name to be presented against the candidate chosen by my opponents. That person was Rod Murphy, who had recently been elected to the House of Commons and had no previous experience in the national party organization.

There had been no organization on my part. Nor did I ask any of my supporters to influence the delegates at the meeting. In fact, many Manitoba delegates did not attend and were not aware of what had been planned. The vote was taken and Murphy was selected.

I accepted the result and did not permit my name to be put in nomination against the selected candidates. Mentally I had made a decision that would change my entire political career. I simply required time to determine whether this decision should be implemented.

For several days I pondered the issue. The question of future participation in the NDP was at a crossroads. I had previously told the trade union movement that I could not possibly support anti-scab legislation.

It was also apparent that a new power structure within the NDP would not tolerate my opinions, particularly those related to affirmative action, militant feminism and interventionist labour legislation. As far as I was concerned there was no longer any avenue within the party for me to fight these issues.

Instead of fighting against those challenges, I found himself constantly supporting those same colleagues in the legislature. I realized that if I was to mount a challenge, it would have to be from the outside. Otherwise I would be required to abandon the positions that had drawn me into politics in the first place. I had no choice but to put all my eggs in one basket.

Either way there was a risk. I could win or lose everything. I made my decision. Upon returning to Winnipeg, I made one last appearance as a speaker at a NDP function. At that gathering Murphy went out of his way to praise me for my past activities in the party and in particular my continued efforts on behalf of northern Manitoba.

I did not acknowledge what I considered to be a hypocritical endorsement and made a speech which essentially attacked the party's trend to abandon the concept of free collective bargaining.

I prepared my resignation from the New Democratic Party caucus. I would continue to sit in the legislature as an independent New Democrat. After I reviewed the document with my wife and two sons, who had been active in my political career, they agreed that I had to do it this way or no way. I then called a press conference on December 4, 1979 where I made the following statement:

> "At its last two conventions the New Democratic Party adopted a policy which would make it illegal for a person to try to hire anyone if his regular employees stop work collectively in an attempt to improve their conditions of employment.
> Legislation of this kind was urged on the government when we were in office and was denied. It was contrary to both party policy and the government's objective of pursuing freedom rather than compounding restrictions in laws affecting industrial disputes.

My personal views in this regard were completely consistent with our previous policy and I cannot in conscience support the reversal of that policy.. It has always been my view that attempts to solve industrial disputes through government control will always work to the detriment of employees. Permitting employees to exercise the same freedom as other citizens enjoy will be to their ultimate advantage. But freedom is indivisible and restrictions cannot be legally imposed on employers without ultimately affecting employees.

It is not unusual for people in the same party to differ philosophically. Usually such differences co-exist.

In this case however a concerted group of individuals has indicated its determination to remove me from any position of influence within the party.

They have initiated the following actions.

1. Past and present officials of the MFL have indicated to various people that they intend to unseat me in my constituency and have attempted unsuccessfully to recruit someone to challenge me.

2. The current president of the MFL wrote a letter to Ed Schreyer when he was still party leader, indicating that union members were having difficulty supporting the party because of me. Mr. Schreyer rejected this contention.

3. This same group has continued its efforts to reduce and ultimately eliminate my effectiveness and at the recent national convention succeeded in organizing a move to remove me as a National Vice-President.

These events do not only affect me personally. They are intended to convey the message that anyone who stands up vigorously against policies considered important to some in the Trade Union movement will be displaced from any position of importance within the party.

I cannot continue as an effective representative under these conditions. I cannot be a participant to an organization in which a controlling group is determined to undermine me.

I do not intend to let myself be steadily removed from public life by my own confederates. Neither do I intend to quit.

My actions now are determined by two factors:

1. I cannot support a position which is completely contrary to the fundamental principles of freedom.

2. An atmosphere has been and is being created that makes it impossible to be effective in the party if one does not accept the position of one group within organized labour.

I had hoped for some time that the matter would solve itself with the passage of time. I now see that as time goes on there is no improvement. On the contrary the situation steadily deteriorates.

I am accordingly going to advise the Speaker of the House that I will henceforth not be a member of the New Democratic Party group in the legislature. I am also resigning from the party.

Since I have not abandoned any of the principles which drew me into public life I will continue to represent my constituency as an Independent New Democrat and I will so present myself in the next election.

I wish to make it clear that I have full confidence that no active member of my constituency has participated in or supported the actions directed against me which I described."

The media greeted the announcement with genuine surprise and gave it prominence. Party caucus members, particularly Sam Uskiw, expressed their understanding and disappointment. On the other hand, opponents quickly got into the act and ensured that the media reported their comments, which could be summarized as 'good riddance to bad rubbish'.

Generally dismayed with my action, party members made numerous telephone calls to the NDP headquarters for several weeks. Those who called were told that I had not resigned and no formal resignation had been reviewed. When one of the callers told me about the response, I immediately got in touch with the NDP office and told them that I had personally handed my resignation to party leader Howard Pawley. This was an official act and party members should not be misled as to my status.

I then met with my Inkster constituents who were genuinely disappointed and distressed by my action. With regret they accepted my explanation. Some attempted to have Pawley discuss the matter with me, but the reality was clear. Those who supported Pawley and had influence over him, were pleased to see me out of the way.

In the ensuing months, I sat as an independent. On several occasions I enabled New Democrats to accomplish certain objectives which their own caucus was unable to achieve. In particular, when Jim Walding, the NDP spokesman on hydro issues, received a leaked document which was rather embarrassing to the Conservative administration, he was challenged by Premier Sterling Lyon, who questioned the validity of the document.

When Pawley tried to debate the issue he was ruled out of order. I rose on a matter of privilege. Since the Premier had indicated a member was using a forged document the question of privileges of the House was at stake and the member was entitled to debate that question. In a rare ruling, the Speaker upheld my position and the debate was permitted to proceed.

During the debate I produced a document obtained in an acceptable manner. It was handwritten by Manitoba Hydro solicitor Stewart Martin. The same handwriting appeared on the document produced by Walding. Both were written by Martin. While Martin remained noncommittal there was no doubt it was his document and he was happy that it was revealed.

The Lyon administration had appointed George Tritschler, a former Chief Justice of Manitoba, to conduct an inquiry into the NDP government's actions in regard to the Nelson River development. Tritschler delivered a report which appeared to be highly critical of the government's conduct.

No one in the NDP caucus had either read or understood the report. I took up the cudgel on behalf of the former government. I spent several hours in debate showing that the Tritschler report either supported the NDP's activity or was blatantly wrong. After the debate Pawley publicly acknowledged the member for Inkster for successfully showing that the inquiry did not find fault with the NDP's development of the Nelson River. I had closed my address by giving a title to the Tritschler report, which I predicted would go on the shelves of some government library. I called it the "Tritschler Report into Power Energy." Despite the tendency to identify documents by their initials nobody appeared to pick up the fact that I had labeled the Tritschler report as TRIPE.

While I was sitting as an Independent New Democrat, a number of meetings were organized where some prominent New Democrats signed a document indicating it would be to the long-term benefit of the party not to nominate a candidate in Inkster to run against me. In several weeks of meetings the petition was signed by more than 100 people, including four former NDP presidents, several vice-presidents and other party dignitaries.

The petition was made public at a press conference on April 14, 1980. When contacted by the media, NDP president Bob Mayer said the document was irrelevant. With thousands of members, the opinions of a hundred was of no consequence to him.

The lines were drawn. It was apparent that the New Democrats would try to defeat me at the next election.

THE PROGRESSIVES

From the date of my defection from the NDP in December 1979 until the spring of 1981 I continued as the Independent New Democrat in the legislature. I was also involved in an active legal practice which found me arguing cases in the Manitoba courts and the Supreme Court of Canada.

After some initial attempts at reconciliation, the NDP set about to find a challenger for the Inkster riding. The initial choice was Roland Penner, a Winnipeg lawyer and professor at the U of M law school, but he declined. In the end the challenge came from a relatively unknown New Democrat, Donald Scott. It was widely speculated that, running as an Independent New Democrat, I would win the seat and subsequently attempts would be made to reconcile my differences with the party.

In the meantime Howard Pawley made an announcement that the so-called anti-scab legislation was being placed on the back burner. Thus the measure which led to my defection was being quietly withdrawn and those who had promised to enact this legislation in order to advance their positions, had been shown to be unreliable.

The situation did not improve. In the Legislature, my role was directed towards discrediting the Lyon government. But any progress in this regard was to the benefit of the New Democrats, the official opposition.

I realized my own participation was not likely to change the current direction of the NDP. Given my philosophy that the public votes for or against a government, and if they vote against a government, they will choose the party most likely to form the government, my position became untenable. This ultimately led to a new and dramatic development.

Within the New Democratic Party there were still many people who adhered to the concepts that had previously determined the party's direction and were totally opposed to the new direction initiated by the trade union movement and militant feminists. The Pawley/Cowan/McBryde forces had successfully rid themselves of their nemesis but this was not enough. Others remained who opposed their course of action and particularly those who still believed I would be an asset to the party and continued to register their objection to the manner in which I had been eliminated.

As far as the powers in the party were concerned, these people would also have to go. Number one on their list was Ben Hanuschak. He had entered the legislature with me in 1966 and had worked with me in an effort to set new directions for the party. The former provincial secretary was the only caucus member to support me in the 1968 leadership campaign.

After my defection, Hanuschak continued to register his opinions in the caucus. That did not sit well with Cowan and other Pawley supporters, including the party bureaucracy. Those individuals, along with trade union activists, initiated a move to unseat Hanuschak in Burrows in the next election.

New Democrats considered Burrows to be a safe seat. However they apparently ignored the fact that, when Hanuschak first ran, a nominating meeting could not be convened because of the lack of NDP membership in the riding. Hanuschak subsequently defeated a distinguished and well-established Liberal, Mark Smerchansky.

Now Hanuschak was considered to be expendable and steps were taken to wrest the nomination from him. The veteran was vulnerable because he had not maintained a strong personal following in Burrows, understandably working on the premise that his performance and the presence of many New Democrats in the riding would be sufficient for him to carry the day. In any event he was completely at odds with the new direction taken by the party.

The other member whose favorable opinion of me caused anxiety within the caucus was Bud Boyce, the member for Winnipeg Centre. A teacher at St. John's Technical High School, he had not been politically active until the 1966 election. In the following election he won the nomination in Winnipeg Centre. That riding, which in four previous elections had been represented by Conservative James Cowan, was not considered winnable, but with the surging support for the New Democratic Party, he was elected and sat as a backbencher for several years. Because of his obvious intelligence, Schreyer was finally persuaded to give him a cabinet post.

Known to have supported me both in 1968 and 1969, his continued outspoken comments which generally favoured my approach were viewed with alarm by other caucus members. Although no active plans were made to replace him in Winnipeg Centre the writing was on the wall as far as his future with the NDP was concerned.

Considering the attitude within the party towards these members and the untenability of my position – since my strategy of trying to change the direction of the party through my own defection had little impact – I was compelled to consider an alternative. After discussions with Boyce and Hanuschak, a meeting was convened. It was attended by Hanuschak, Boyce, Wally Johannson – a former MLA who was also disturbed by the party's new direction – Murdoch MacKay – a former NDP president – and Max Hofford – a former vice-president. The meeting was held in the cellar of Boyce's west-end home, an appropriate location for a revolutionary conspiracy. At the meeting five of the six men decided to form a new political party, which would be called the Progressives. Johannson was sympathetic with the intentions but his profound loyalty to the NDP, to whom he had devoted his adult life, kept him from going along. He did not sign the Progressive Charter.

It was decided that Hanuschak would announce his departure from the New Democratic Party in the legislature. Accordingly on February 26, 1981, he rose and made a statement, giving reasons for his defection and indicating he wished to be a part of a socialist party. Boyce was to make a similar announcement the following day, but he simply told the press that he too was leaving the NDP caucus.

On March 3, 1981 I held a press conference announcing the formation of the Progressive Party of Manitoba. I read the Charter which stipulated:

> "There is now constituted the Progressive Party of Manitoba.
>
> The Party is dedicated to the principle that the public through its elected representatives has a major responsibility for the creation of a climate conducive to the betterment of the human condition.
>
> The political objective of the Party is to form the Government of Manitoba.
>
> The present platform of the Party includes the following:
> - Sound public industrial development,
> - freedom of collective bargaining for employees and employers,
> - fiscal responsibility,
> - excess profits tax on resource industries,
> - full employment.
>
> The founding members of the Party are Max Hofford, Murdoch MacKay, Bud Boyce, Ben Hanuschak and Sidney Green.
>
> Each of the founding members is prepared to be a candidate in the next provincial election."

The creation of the Progressive Party was greeted with mixed reactions by the media but the announcement was given due recognition because of its startling nature and the involvement of three members of the legislative assembly. Unprecedented in the history of Manitoba, it was treated accordingly.

From the date the Progressive party was formed, the members played a significant role in the legislature. They underlined their differences from the New Democratic Party by moving amendments during debates on throne speech and the budget. They also introduced resolutions which were in line with what had previously been NDP policy. In particular, they introduced a resolution which called for the government to remove itself from accepting revenues from gambling. Interestingly enough, Howard Pawley and Saul Cherniack both voted against this resolution even though it was entirely in accordance with NDP policy and their own previously expressed opinions.

As indicated by New Democratic Party sources, the party was unlikely to support any resolutions brought forward by the Progressives even if they were totally in accordance with their own policy. Such proved to be the case.

Speculation then centered around MLA Sam Uskiw. If he became the fourth Progressive member, the party would achieve official status in the legislature. It was generally understood that Uskiw supported the position of the Progressive position since he made public remarks in that direction after the party was formed.

Uskiw and I never discussed the subject. I believed that, if Uskiw was to move, he had to move on his own. Finally Uskiw did make a public announcement to the effect that he would try to change the direction of the New Democratic Party from within. He subsequently made several speeches throughout the province expressing apprehension about the direction in which the NDP was moving. For this Uskiw ultimately paid a price. As indicated earlier, he was shunned by the NDP establishment even though Pawley was compelled to bring this veteran into his cabinet.

Ultimately Uskiw left the party and now is a major consultant and contributor to the Conservative party. He also addressed Progressive Party meetings during election campaigns and indicated the extent to which the New Democratic Party had become a captive of the trade union movement. He said that none of his appointments as minister became effective until approved by the Manitoba Federation of Labour.

The stated objective of the Progressive Party was to form a government. I continued to believe that in an election the public will vote either for or against the party in power. If they want to vote against the government they vote for the party which is most likely to defeat the government. According to my formula, in order to obtain electoral support, the political party must be clear and articulate in expressing its position so the people can accept it as an alternative to the government.

The task of achieving that goal was Herculean since the New Democrats had twenty representatives in the Legislature, while the Progressives had only three. As well, the NDP had gained a tremendous amount of respect through the efforts of everyone who had contributed to it, including the three defectors. On the other hand, the Progressives were a fledgling group, largely suspected as banding together because of sour grapes on the part of some individuals.

Initially the Progressives made substantial gains. They were the first to declare candidates for the expected 1981 election, as the five founders registered. In a short time they were joined by another four candidates. A press conference was held to announce the candidacy of George Simpson, Joel Morassutte, David Birchard and Pat Bazan. The struggle for candidates was difficult, but the Progressives soon had more candidates in the field than any other party.

Those first candidates were screened with respect to their acceptance, but the party was criticized by New Democrats because it did not have constituency organizations which held nominating meetings. The critics had apparently forgotten that, before and including 1966, the NDP had fielded many candidates in seats where no constituency nominating meetings had been held. Instead candidates were parachuted into ridings with last-minute struggles to obtain the required number of names on the nomination document. When I entered the legislature, the NDPs nominated 53 candidates. (for the 57 seat House). The Progressives would ultimately nominate 36.

As far as the Progressives were concerned, the most important factor was time. It was our objective to have 57 candidates. If the party was successful in nominating people in every constituency it would be entitled to receive the recognition that such a field of candidates inspires.

If this recognition occurred it would not be necessary to have a big campaign fund since the daily Progressive announcements, as reported by the media, would be more attractive and newsworthy than those made by other parties. News reports would be far more effective than expensive advertising but the strategy depended on the nomination of close to 57 candidates. At least one year from the formation of the party was required. Unfortunately for the Progressives, Lyon called an election for November 17, 1981.

No doubt Lyon believed his main opposition was in disarray and the NDP vote would be split, thereby providing him with an easy victory. But he failed to take into account the hostility to his government. It was so intense, the public wanted to ensure it would not remain in power.

This worked in favour of the New Democrats and against me. The election was called. The Progressives had named only 19 candidates. While they eventually had 36 candidates, there were 57 ridings and the media did not consider the Progressives as a party in contention and treated them accordingly.

The struggle to obtain candidates between the issuing of the election writ and the deadline for nominations was intense. All attempts at screening were abandoned. In particular I remember receiving a call from Boyce, who was in charge of the campaign office. Boyce had a person who wished to run for the Elmwood constituency. His name was Curtis Bloodworth. I asked, "what is he like?" Boyce responded, "He's breathing." I said, "Take him on."

Despite such desperate last-minute attempts, the Progressives did field some exceptionally strong candidates, including four former MLAs and other distinguished members of the community. They had a policy and conducted a vigorous campaign.

Since there were no constituency organizations, the campaign centered around a series of meetings in the areas where the party had fielded candidates. At each meeting I produced new material, copies of which were submitted to the media.

However the needed publicity was not forthcoming. This spelled disaster because the Progressives' advertising budget was very limited and their dependence on their policy position was vital. The absence of media reports about their activities was fatal. It is significant that a party with 36 candidates whose leader spoke at a public meeting almost every day did not receive a single voice clip on the CBC.

The CBC policy is worthy of mention. On the Friday before the election the CBC made what it described as an unannounced news poll. On the six o'clock news, Manitobans were asked to phone in their preference for the election, which would then be tabulated. Phone calls would be received from six to seven o'clock. The CBC announced that none of the parties had been notified beforehand of the plan. The secrecy was intended to prevent organized phone calls.

Calls started pouring in from all over the province. The results indicated that the New Democrats were receiving the highest percentage of this informal poll with the Conservatives trailing behind them. The Progressives received approximately two per cent. During the program CBC announced it would continue to receive calls beyond the originally stated cut-off time. After that time more calls came in which ultimately gave the Conservatives a higher percentage than the NDP.

Instead of making the final figures public, the CBC released only the numbers related to calls received during the originally scheduled time frame. This decision clearly favoured the New Democrats. Many people believe election polls have an effect on the final result but this assessment is debatable.

I was suspicious about why the CBC had not announced the final result. Both I and the Conservatives criticized this decision. Following the election, CBC apparently wanted to vindicate itself and planned a program dealing with the criticism which it had received.

I was called to participate in the program which would focus on the role of the media in election campaigns. I readily agreed and arrived at the CBC studio on the Friday following the election. Nate Nurgitz, the Conservative organizer who subsequently became a senator and now is a Queen's Bench Judge, was also asked to participate.

When I arrived I was told that the program would be taped for a half hour but only ten minutes would be shown. I did not want to participate in such a program since the allotted time was insufficient to properly cover the subject. I also objected to editing of the tape. I was ready to leave the studio when producer Marv Terhoff said he was willing to negotiate. I did not wish to negotiate. Terhoff then said the program would be 15 minutes with no editing and urged me to stay. I agreed and joined Nurgitz, four representatives of the media and host John Harvard, who now is a Liberal member of Parliament for Winnipeg South Centre.

Harvard announced the program as "Media bashing on one." I immediately rose and said had not come to participate in a such program since I did not engage in any media bashing. A retake was done and Harvard announced the program as the "Responsibility of the media in an election campaign."

During the taping I said I could not disagree with the media reporting the news as they saw it. But I did disagree with the media creating a self-fulfilling scenario and taking a specific direction during the election campaign. As an example I noted the reporting of the CBC polling results. In my view the reported results had deliberately favoured the NDP. I also suspected that New Democrats had previous knowledge of the poll and its time frame because their phone-in campaign was strongest during the originally scheduled hour. I noted the activity stopped after the hour because they were not aware the original cut-off had been extended. I believed this would explain why the Conservatives, who apparently did not know beforehand of the original time frame, won the poll in the extended time.

I then said that the CBC announced a false result. Anyone involved in similar action in the legislature would have been required to resign. I called on those CBC personnel responsible for the poll to behave accordingly.

Quite satisfied with the interview, I went home to see it. It was scheduled to appear on the 6:30 news but the item was conspicuous by its absence. It was never shown. It may still be in the CBC archives. The CBC's excuse for not showing it was because it I had dominated the piece.

In the 1981 election the Progressives received only two per cent of the vote. The three MLAs were defeated. Hanuschak and I each received eight hundred votes, less than 10 per cent of the total vote in our respective constituencies.

The New Democrats won the election with the largest popular vote the party had ever received. If my efforts in the campaign had any effect, it was to further discredit the Conservatives to the benefit of the NDP.

The NDP establishment was jubilant. They had not only won the election but had soundly trashed the internal opposition. Herb Schultz, who had been sympathetic to the issues which had led to my defection from the New Democratic Party, insisted he could reform the party from within. He spent about two years trying to achieve that goal but his effort was totally futile in the face of the NDP's electoral success.

Initially Schultz was merely regarded as a pain in the neck by the New Democrats, but as someone who did not shy away from any intimidation or attempts to embarrass him, his attacks intensified. Ultimately he was expelled from the party by a formal resolution at a party convention in February 1984. That was probably an unprecedented act in the annals of political party histories in Canada.

The Progressives were routed. I resigned himself to devoting my energies to the practice of law. I also pledged to continue working with the Progressives to maintain its presence on the Manitoba political landscape. It would be a fringe group devoted to articulating certain distinctive ideas.

DECLINE OF PROGRESSIVE PARTY

Between the 1981 provincial election and 1995 the Progressives experienced a slow decline. Despite a poor showing in 1981, Progressive candidates showed remarkable resilience. At meetings held within weeks after the vote, they vowed to continue their efforts. Taking a cautious approach, I suggested the party continue as an educational group which would hold monthly meetings to deal with topics of current political interest.

This approach was adopted and for some years the party held fairly well-attended dinner meetings at a restaurant in north Winnipeg. They usually featured guest speakers and involved subjects of current concern. Speakers included Jack London, dean of the Manitoba Law School, and Mayor Bill Norrie.

The next electoral opportunity occurred when a by-election was called for October 2, 1984 in Fort Garry. I was the candidate for the Progressive and conducted a vigorous campaign in a race which featured the entry into the political scene of the newly elected Liberal Leader Sharon Carstairs. I came within 100 votes of the NDP candidate but the Conservative party was the winner. While the results were disappointing the slightly more than 1,000 votes received by me was much higher than usually experienced by a candidate of a new and unestablished party.

In the general election of 1986 the Progressives ran 12 candidates all of whom were soundly defeated. I contested Wolseley, the constituency where I reside and drew only 4.3 per cent of the vote. In a previous by-election on October 1, 1985 Ben Hanuschak ran in Kildonan. Despite a credible campaign he received only 6 per cent of the vote.

The NDP victory in 1986 was short-lived. Howard Pawley's administration had barely scraped back to power after completing its first term with no substantial record of achievement. The highlight or nadir of the first term involved the French language issue. The Societe Franco-Manitobaine had supported a law suit which claimed that the Manitoba's statute which made English the official language of the province was unconstitutional, and the law of Canada required all the province's statutes to be printed in English and French.

Manitoba Attorney-General Roland Penner attempted to negotiate a compromise to meet the group's complaints and prevent a court ruling. He presented a constitutional amendment to the Legislature which called for the entrenchment of the French language in Manitoba.

I had long been a proponent of the official use of French and English in Canada and in the province. As a Cabinet minister I was one of the few whose door and designation were printed in both languages. I had frequently been interviewed in French and made speeches to French-speaking audiences. However I was adamantly opposed to the entrenchment proposed by the Pawley administration and publicly made my opinions known on many occasions.

My position on this issue was consistent with my position on entrenchment of rights generally. I was one of the few politicians who opposed the Trudeau Charter of Rights. In a speech to the legislative committee I argued that the Charter of Rights gave nine unelected judges the right to enact social and economic laws, which would be binding on the country, and could not be overruled by the legislature. In my view, it was a denial of rights, not a protector of rights.

In November 1980 a committee of Manitoba Legislature heard representations concerning the Charter of Rights and Freedoms. I made a presentation wherein I demonstrated that the Charter did not confer rights but rather inhibited the democratic process. CBC journalist Jack Kusch gave the following critique:

> "The most effective submission came from independent MLA Sid Green, who cited American precedence showing how a supreme court could undermine the political will of the nation and cut off effective debate on policy issues.
>
> Independent MLA Sid Green made the most forceful appearance before the Legislative Committee on the Constitution."

My prophecy proved to be correct. More and more politicians are questioning the validity of having delegated social, economic and political power to nine judges who are electorally responsible to no one.

Roy Romanow, former premier of Saskatchewan, was actively involved in getting the Charter enacted. After it was enacted Romanow made a speech in which he questioned the wisdom of what had been done. He said no politicians had registered warnings that the Charter might be used to give the courts an opportunity to inhibit socially progressive legislation.

I reminded Romanow of my own comments to the legislative committee. Later when addressing the Canadian Club in Winnipeg, Romanow noted my presence and changed his address to indicate that "very few" politicians had indicated the danger that would result from the enactment of the Charter of Rights.

The constitutional amendment regarding the use of the French language caused an uproar in the Manitoba legislature and led to a situation which can best be described by the song "The Bells are Ringing." In both the federal and Manitoba legislatures the Speaker summons the members for a vote by ringing bells which can be heard throughout the building. In late 1983 and early 1984, bell-ringing became a regular event in the Manitoba legislature as the Conservatives utilized every method to prevent passage of the constitutional amendment.

Even the replacement of government House Leader Roland Penner with Andy Anstett, who had been a former deputy clerk of the assembly and had extensive knowledge about how to use the rules, and subsequent attempts to make the government's action more palatable, failed to sway the opposition. The Conservatives continued to walk out of the chamber when a recorded vote was called and the division bells rang until the end of the sitting each day.

The final straw occurred when Anstett tried to convince Speaker Jim Walding to limit the time the bells could ring. When the Speaker refused, the House Leader introduced a motion of privilege which called for a two-hour limit on the ringing. Unfortunately, while on other issues the bells could only ring until the end of that day's sitting, on a matter of privilege they could ring indefinitely.

Therefore when Anstett introduced the motion, the Conservatives walked out and stayed out for eleven days. During that time, the premier wrote to the Speaker virtually ordering him to call a vote – with or without the Conservatives in the Chamber. The Speaker declined. Ultimately the government surrendered, the House was prorogued and the issue died on the order paper.

Speaker Walding's refusal to put the question to a vote when the Conservatives refused to respond to the bells was an incredible decision but it confirmed what had been the practice in the House. Bell ringing was simply supposed to give all members fair warning of a pending vote. It was never intended that failure to respond to the bells would enable a minority to veto government legislation. The Pawley government had neither the strength nor the inclination to force the Speaker's hand and ultimately abandoned the legislation.

The Speaker's reaction to the premier's request was contrary to all parliamentary traditions. It is inconceivable that a minority could prevent action by a duly elected government by refusing to respond to the division bells.

The Speaker should simply have given the members a reasonable opportunity to return and then conducted a vote. A similar incident occurred when I was the NDP government House leader. Attempting to keep the government from continuing with its legislative program, the Conservatives refused to answer the bell.

After waiting for more than half an hour – then an unprecedented length of time – I went to the Speaker Peter Fox's office and said that in my view the Speaker should give the Conservatives a reasonable length of time to return. If they did not return, I said the Speaker should advise the Opposition of his intention to reconvene the legislature. Fox responded by suggesting this action was contrary to the rules and customs of the House. He had no alternative but wait until the Opposition advised him that the members were ready for the vote.

I challenged the statement, saying the Speaker should convey to the Conservatives the House leader's position with respect to taking a vote and, if the vote was not taken, I would put another member in the chair to act as Speaker and conduct the vote.

Accordingly the Speaker communicated that message to Conservative Leader Sidney Spivak. Shortly thereafter the Conservatives returned to the chamber and parliamentary procedure continued as usual. It is unfortunate that neither the federal nor the Manitoba government had the gumption and courage to persist in a parliamentary program in later years. Instead they permitted the minority opposition to frustrate the democratic process.

In any event in Manitoba the Opposition's tactics resulted in the legislation being withdrawn while the Pawley administration, which was under severe public attack, attempted to rectify its position.

In the next session, Anstett, who was responsible for the French language legislation, modified the program to eliminate its objectionable features and it was passed.

The Pawley government miraculously succeeded in being re-elected in 1986 but it was to be a short-lived victory. During its first four years in office the government had not produced any major achievements and persisted in a fiscal program which was spelling disaster for the financial stability of the province.

In 1988 I was in Australia when I received a telephone call from Winnipeg, advising me that the government had been defeated. Walding, who had been demoted to a backbencher, voted against the government's budgetary program. I was also told that the election would be held on April 26, 1988. Pawley had resigned and the New Democrats intended to have a leadership convention during the election campaign.

The NDP sought to recreate the same impetus which the party had gained in 1969 when Schreyer and I ran for the leadership during the campaign.

It was also announced that whoever would become leader would also be named the premier for the last two weeks of the provincial election race since he would be the leader of the majority party. It has always been the case in Canada that when a prime minister resigns and a new leader is chosen, that person takes over the title because he commands majority support in the Parliament.

However it was completely without precedent to name a person as prime minister or premier when there was no legislative assembly, as was the case in Manitoba. The House had been dissolved for the election.

I returned to Manitoba in early March and called a meeting of the Progressives to see whether they would participate in the contest. Members decided to participate and nominated six candidates.

In the meantime no political figure or member of the media questioned the fact that if Gary Doer was elected as the NDP leader, he would become the premier. This was taken for granted. At a Progressive meeting I announced that I would get in touch with the Lieutenant-Governor of Manitoba, George Johnson, a former Conservative MLA and cabinet minister, and complain about that issue. My letter, delivered on March 27, 1988, read as follows:

"There are public reports to the effect that Premier Howard Pawley will be tendering his resignation and requesting that you appoint either Conrad Santos, Gary Doer, Maureen Hemphill, Andy Anstett or Leonard Harapiak to be the premier of Manitoba. I regard this proposed action as incredulous but wish to register my objection on the assumption that the reports are true.

The representative of the Queen is empowered to choose a First Minister, and parliamentary convention suggests that he does so by choosing that person who can claim the support of Parliament or the Legislature. None of the persons named can claim such support as they presently are not members of the Legislative Assembly.

It would appear that the request is being made to you not to facilitate a head of government being appointed but rather to facilitate an election campaign in which it is sought to have one of these people masquerading about the Province as Premier.

I know of no precedent whereby a Premier has been chose in the midst of an election campaign. I respectfully suggest that, if there is such a precedent, it is wrong and should be ignored.

There is no reason that the present government should not continue unchanged until April 26, 1988 when you will be able to determine which person should be called upon to form a government.

I respectfully suggest that you should not permit yourself to be manipulated for partisan political purposes. In the event that Mr. Pawley tenders his resignation to you, I respectfully suggest that he be advised that if accepted, he will have no assurance that you will make the appointment that he anticipates. Instead I suggest that he be informed that he is to continue as First Minister until a new government is chosen. If he insists on resigning, there are numerous options available to yourself other than that which is being requested of you.

It has been suggested in news reports that the conduct of the Premier and your desired response would be legal. Although this may be so, it does not follow that what is legal is desirable. In any event the procedure which is hereby being suggested is also legal.

I trust you will give this letter your earnest consideration."

The media had a new story and my letter was given prominence. Shortly thereafter the Liberals adopted the same position with respect to Doer although Sharon Carstairs declined to speak on the subject. The stories, public criticism and controversy which followed my letter resulted in Pawley remaining as premier during the election campaign.

The NDP campaign demonstrated the futility of its position. A concurrent leadership campaign did nothing to enhance the party's chances and merely demonstrated the weaknesses of the Pawley government and its poor management of the province.

Following the defeat in the chamber, the party bureaucracy, who knew Pawley could not win public support, urged him to resign. After Doer became leader, the campaign tried to demonstrate that, with him at the helm, the party was distancing itself from the Pawley government. The NDP ran on the slogan "New Direction, New Leadership" – in fact 'new everything'. This prompted me to comment during a Peter Warren show that the New Democratic Party government was the first incumbent government to run on the slogan "It's time for a change."

The New Democrats were soundly defeated and Conservative Gary Filmon became the premier. However, his victory was a narrow one, with only 25 seats in the 57-seat legislature. The Liberals, led by Carstairs, made a strong resurgence and captured 20 seats while the NDP won 12 seats.

The Progressives continued to field candidates in various elections and by-elections during the 1980s and early 1990s. It had no political success and could only claim that it had garnered more votes than any other "fourth" party which appeared from time to time on the political scene. The strongest showing was in the Crescentwood by-election where I received almost 1,000 votes, enough to qualify for 50 per cent public financing of the campaign.

Receiving such public funding was a paradox. The law permitted the government to use public funds to finance the election campaign of any candidate or party which won more than 10 per cent of the votes in any constituency.

The Progressives had challenged the law in Manitoba courts on the basis that it forced citizens to finance political beliefs which they did not support. Indeed the basis of this challenge was similar to the challenge made against the public financing of private and religious schools. The challenge was unsuccessful in the Court of Queen's Bench but received a dissenting judgment from Mr. Justice Huband in the Manitoba Court of Appeal.

Leave was granted to appeal to the Supreme Court of Canada where I, accompanied by Murdoch MacKay, who was also a petitioner, argued the case. The Supreme Court declined to answer the critical question as to whether the legislation was legal and dismissed the appeal on the rather surprising condition that there was no factual foundation to substantiate the action.

This issue had never been raised in the lower courts. It was accepted that the petitioners were taxpayers and their tax funds were used to finance political campaigns. Because this case was not decided on its merits this issue may be reheard by the Supreme Court when some person or group objects to seeing their tax money being used to finance political beliefs that they totally oppose.

Nevertheless the Progressive party did receive a 50 per cent public financing for an election campaign. From time to time I was asked how the party could take this money when it was opposed to the legislation. I had no difficulty responding that as long as the rule was in existence, and Progressives were asked to finance Liberals, Conservatives and New Democrats, they would not refuse the reciprocal contributions from members of the other parties. They would however, continue to vigorously oppose the laws which made these contributions mandatory.

Another significant action taken by the Progressives in the courts was a challenge levelled against the NDP government for advertising its programs during the Kildonan by-election campaign in 1985. While the New Democrats had passed a law prohibiting new advertising during an election, they had no difficulty in side-stepping its principle. Indeed, they were the party most guilty of using public monies for propaganda purposes by purchasing extensive newspaper and television advertising, which was blatantly political, during their terms of office.

According to the law, this was not illegal, but when the advertising continued during the campaign, the Progressives decided to test the issue in courts after the chief returning officer rejected their complaint. The court decided against the government on some of the advertising while upholding the right of the government to place advertisements as part of a regular program. Thus the Progressives were the only party to successfully challenge the law, although no consequences ensued since the legislation does not provide for any penalty.

The Progressives continued to hold public meetings which were attended by a hard core of 30 to 40 supporters. Given the lack of electoral success their loyalty was astonishing. The party maintained a contact list of 250 to 300 people who continued to show some interest in its activities.

But the party's electoral position had to be adjusted. My thesis that people vote either for or against the government remained valid, but it ensured that the Progressives would not be in contention because they never fielded enough candidates to form a government.

A new strategy was required with respect to candidates . An idea came to me while my wife and I were on vacation in California. In a restaurant, while waiting for lunch to be served, I took out a paper napkin and started to scribble something that had been gnawing on my mind while driving. I wanted to give voters a reason to elect a Progressive candidate.

I believed the Progressives had a position on several important issues which was distinct from the other parties, but it was difficult to demonstrate the distinctiveness. Satisfied that there was public support for each of the issues, I finally worked out a format. The slogan would be "Which side are you on?"

That slogan was used in Crescentwood by-election and the 1986 general election, as well as in newspaper ads released on a regular basis to highlight party activities. Although it did not receive the kind of positive response that was hoped for, it did more clearly identify the Progressives on Manitoba's political spectrum. The following is an example of Progressive party advertisements using this pitch:

WHICH SIDE ARE YOU ON?

Conservatives, Liberals & NDP say:	Progressives say:
Treat some Manitobans as minorities	Treat all Manitobans as equals
State-imposed labour contracts	Labour contracts freely negotiated
Government must finance some political parties	Government must not finance any political parties
Government gambling houses	No government gambling
Spend more than you have	Balance the budget
Native Indians are nations which should have self-government	Native Indians have self-government as citizens of Canada
Classify Manitobans as male, female, homosexual & lesbian	Manitobans are male or female

If you are on the right side, THE PROGRESSIVES ARE INTERESTED IN YOU!
... and you should be interested in the Progressives.

The last by-election in which the Progressives participated occurred in 1993 in the St. John's constituency. A young Progressive candidate, Neil Schipper, carried the party banner. The "Which side are you on?" slogan was part of the election literature and was advertised extensively.

Schipper received 4.97 per cent of the vote, a disappointing result but almost twice as much as that received by independent candidates in other by-elections.

After that exercise the question arose about the party's position in regard to the next general election, expected in 1995. I called an executive meeting in the fall of 1994. It was attended by about ten party stalwarts.

At the meeting I outlined the difficulties involved with establishing a political party and making its name recognizable. I indicated that, while no Progressives had been elected, the party did have some recognition on the political scene and the Progressive name was included in most public opinion polls.

Nevertheless I believed it was wrong for the party to exist primarily as Sidney Green's party. I was quite willing to work for the party but felt a new leader should be chosen in order to demonstrate that the Progressives were not merely the embodiment of one personality. I also believed that new young leadership should carry the load in the future – if there was a future. Two of the younger members undertook to develop programs to ensure survival. If successful, the party would field candidates in the next election. If however, the youth initiative did not produce results, I indicated there was no point in continuing.

SIDNEY GREEN

Murdoch MacKay and I waited patiently to see whether the youth initiative would be productive. By the time the election was called no activities had been planned by the new group and the party had not continued with its public meetings and advertisements. Accordingly I did not initiate or encourage any participation in the election. And for the first time since its inception there were no Progressive candidates.

That lack of participation was reported by the media who interviewed me. The party had, in fact, died. Because it had fielded no candidates it was officially removed from the list of active political parties in the Province of Manitoba.

It still had funds in its treasury but no attempt was made to use them for any form of political activity. Manitoba legislation requires that when a political party goes out of existence, its funds are transferred to the Government of Manitoba. On July 13, 1995, MacKay and I signed a cheque and sent it to the government, thereby formally ending the Progressive Party of Manitoba.

PART SIX

REFLECTIONS

THE MEDIA

In political science, the news media is referred to as the "fourth estate." This designation recognizes the importance of the media in the democratic process. This status of the media in regard to political importance is not an exaggeration.

Its role in public affairs cannot be overestimated. No politician can survive without recognition by the media. Indeed, the politician who says he does not care if his name is in the newspapers is simply lying, fooling himself or both.

From the time of my entry into politics I appreciated and sought the attention and recognition of the fourth estate. I saw that there was no magic formula for getting media attention. You had to create legitimate news. I made it a rule never to thank a reporter for a good story or rebuke one for what I considered to be unfair treatment.

This is not to say I would not attempt to correct what I thought were incorrect stories by the media. Frequently I would attempt to clear the record if, in my view, the newspapers or electronic media had wrongly stated a position. I would not talk to the reporter directly and complain. Instead I developed a system which I believed permitted me to demonstrate the unfairness.. This philosophy in regard to the treatment of journalists was largely based on the education I received from my friend David Hunt, who helped him in the 1962 and 1965 federal elections.

Hunt was my mentor insofar as public exposure was concerned. He taught me that there was no point in arguing with reporters because, if anything, such arguments would be counter-productive. Hunt's instruction also led to my policy of never thanking a reporter for a good story, which was frequently done by many of my colleagues.

My approach to the media developed mainly because of reporting by the *Winnipeg Free Press* and *Winnipeg Tribune* during the 1965 federal election. In that contest I ran against Bud Sherman and Margaret Konantz in Winnipeg South. A New Democratic Party victory in that riding was considered impossible.

Towards the end of the campaign Sherman, the Conservative candidate, challenged Liberal Konantz to a public debate. No challenge was issued to me. Ignoring the snub, I immediately responded to Sherman's challenge by sending a public letter to the other two candidates, indicating my willingness to take part in the debate.

It was a pre-fax machine era so the letter and a press release were immediately delivered by hand to the newspapers. The following day Konantz responded to Sherman by letter indicating she would not participate in the debate. The *Winnipeg Free Press* and the *Winnipeg Tribune* gave major coverage to that letter but failed to mention my willingness to participate.

I believed my letter was a legitimate news story since Sherman's challenge had made the front page. After giving the matter serious consideration I decided the newspapers paid for the printing of the news that they felt was important and it was their right to do so. However, since I believed I had the same right with regard to the publication of news I devised a news story with the headline "Silence in South Deliberate – Green." I wrote the story as I would have liked a reporter to write it and purchased an ad to convey what I regarded to be an appropriate piece of news, given my participation as a candidate in the campaign.

I also paid to print a letter containing my photograph and an explanation of the reasons for this action, along with details about the story concerning Sherman's initial challenge to a debate, my response and the lack of any mention of that response in the subsequent newspaper story.

The *Free Press* was astute enough to simply print the paid advertisement without comment. The *Winnipeg Tribune*, however, highlighted my advertisement by rebuking me in a leading editorial, suggesting that my attempt to discredit the *Tribune* with the ad was "sorehead" action. As a result I not only printed my ad but received prime editorial space pointing it out.

I used this tactic on several other occasions. When that occurred I usually requested and received contributions to help pay for the ad. I took that approach when the *Free Press* ran a story indicating the Manitoba Development Corporation was hiding losses when, in fact, the reverse was true. The auditor had believed the process could be dealt with in a less negative manner than actually had occurred. I insisted that the losses be fully documented and revealed.

I did the same thing when the *Free Press* published my response to Finance Minister Don Craik's budget in an article headlined "Craik the Fake" in the morning edition. The story was eliminated in the main edition which was delivered to homes. In response I simply paid for an ad which contained the morning paper story, along with a memo indicating I was helping the *Free Press* publish its own story.

My relations with the press were generally good. I had frequent conversations with many of the reporters and often visited the press room. It is fair to say that, during my years in the legislative assembly I received many superlative comments. Examples of the accolades are as follows:

> "Mr. Green's considerable skill has made him the government's most effective debater . . ." – *Winnipeg Free Press, April 10, 1974*

> "He is easily one of the most capable men in public life . . ." – *Winnipeg Tribune*, July 12, 1974

> "What beautiful music for the tax-payer's ear! Here's a politician, a cabinet minister, who refuses to use the huge government PR apparatus." – *Winnipeg Tribune, June 20, 1975*

> "In the persons of Mr. Lyon and former mines minister Sidney Green, Manitoba has two of the most accomplished parliamentarians in Canada. It is a true joy to watch these two square off in wit, procedural astuteness and repartee." – *Winnipeg Tribune, December 2, 1977*

> "Only on the fourth day of debate did style enter the scene when Sidney Green began his condemnation of the great pretenders on the other side . . ." – *Winnipeg Tribune, February 24, 1979*

> "Green's approach was powerful enough to spread from coast to coast within hours and experts deplored the introduction of such a section . . . Even the premier was required to listen . . . " – *Winnipeg Tribune, July 15, 1980*

> "It is no secret that the strongest opposition on many significant issues in the past session came . . . from the now-independent member of the legislature, Sid Green . . ." – *Winnipeg Free Press, December 10, 1980*

After the 1981 election debacle I continued to be interviewed from time to time with respect to major issues related to politics. The last time I appeared as a public figure in any political commentary was in 1995 when the CBC did a short story on the fact that with the lack of participation of the Progressives election campaign, my political career had officially ended.

PERSONALITIES

❖ TOMMY DOUGLAS

T.C. Douglas is the person in politics whom I most admired and who influenced me more than any other person.

I was not formally involved in politics until 1961 when my law partner and I attended a convention in Alberta sponsored by the Canadian Federation of Labour.

Douglas, then the premier of Saskatchewan, was scheduled to address the convention. When he spoke I was electrified. Here was a politician who was aiming for and expounding the means of achieving greater social justice. He made no bones about being a committed democratic socialist. Douglas was also a practical politician and a premier. Completely devoid of personal vanity and self-aggrandizement, he was unselfishly committed to bringing about social change for the benefit of people.

Tommy Douglas led a very private life. He had few, if any, close associates other than his wife. He was not one to socialize with colleagues after a meeting over dinner or a few drinks. Few got to know Tommy Douglas personally.

I was fortunate to have several one-on-one encounters with Douglas during my political life, partly because I was president of the Manitoba New Democratic Party and on the executive as a vice-president of the national party.

On one occasion Tommy Douglas was staying at the Hotel Fort Garry and I offered to drive him to the airport. Because his plane was late I spent about 45 minutes talking with him. Douglas talked about his career as premier of Saskatchewan.

For instance, he gave me the inside story of an ill-fated box factory, for which his government had been criticized. It had taken over the business which subsequently failed. Douglas said that his government had not intended to get involved in that business but took such action when a union attempted to obtain certification of the factory employees and the matter was pending before the labour board.

The company owner personally got in touch with Douglas and prevailed on him to obtain an adjournment from the board in order to give the owner more time to prepare his case. Once the adjournment was granted, the owner initiated corporate changes which shifted ownership of the factory to a new corporation. Because the law in Saskatchewan at that time did not cover such an eventuality, it appeared the owner had successfully prevailed upon Tommy Douglas to defeat the certification application. The owner obviously did not know Tommy Douglas.

Douglas immediately got his government to expropriate the box factory. The moral of the story was you couldn't fool around with him. Businessmen in Saskatchewan got the message that he would not permit them to violate the spirit or the letter of the law respecting trade union organizations.

Douglas also told me what occurred with respect to Clarence Fines, a finance minister who had been criticized for making money on Saskatchewan bonds.

When the CCF came to power in Saskatchewan, the government implemented a bond issue in order to deal with a large deficit which it had inherited from the Liberal administration. When the financial community expressed concern about the instability of these bonds, Fines announced he would personally buy them to demonstrate confidence in the economic future of the province. Ultimately the bonds made money and Fines made money. It was perfectly legitimate and the minister had done nothing for which he could be properly criticized.

In 1961 Douglas was urged to contest the leadership of the new federal New Democratic Party which had been led by Hazen Argue, a Saskatchewan MP. As a measure of his commitment to social change, Douglas left the premiership in order to lead a party, which as the CCF, had only eight seats in the House of Commons.

Tommy Douglas fought tremendous election campaigns and was the greatest speaker that I had ever witnessed. He asked nothing for himself and fully participated in party conventions and other party activities. In my view he was the most dedicated and most able political figure in Canada during the latter half of the 20th century.

❖ DOUGLAS CAMPBELL

Douglas Campbell was elected to the Manitoba Legislature as a Progressive in 1922. The Progressives were an ad hoc party without a real leader but in that election they won a majority of seats. Since none of their candidates could claim the premiership by virtue of being the leader of the party, the caucus chose one. Campbell was a candidate but the ultimate victor was John Bracken who served as premier of Manitoba from 1922 to 1943.

After Bracken's departure and until 1957 Campbell was the premier and leader of the Liberal Progressive party, as it was then known. He became premier when Bracken went to Ottawa to assume leadership of what he insisted be known as the Progressive Conservative Party. Both men insisted the word "progressive" remain as part of the name of the parties which they led.

Campbell continued as an MLA until 1969 and would probably have been re-elected if he had run. However he stepped aside to make room for Bobby Bend, who had been chosen as leader of the Liberal party after the resignation of Gil Molgat. Ironically, Bend was defeated.

Without question Campbell was the most politically conservative politician I knew during my years in politics. His conservatism was totally philosophical and his power of oratory and logic was so convincing that Conservative members of the Legislature virtually drooled every time he addressed the House, even though he sat in opposition to them.

Campbell continued advocating his philosophical conservatism and became an active member of the Reform party when he was in his 90's. He was in constant demand as a public speaker until his death in 1995 at the age of 99 years and 11 months.

During my years in the legislature and until Campbell's death, I developed a very close relationship with him, even though we appeared to be at opposite ends of the political spectrum. In fact, our views were very similar, with one small but vital distinction. Campbell was conservative and believed that, if every citizen was provided with complete social security they would lose the incentive to produce the kind of results required if they had no security and had to work for it. I, on the other hand, believed that if people were secure and free from economic disadvantage they would be free to develop themselves to their utmost level and therefore make the greatest contribution to society. On all other points related to civil rights, bureaucracy and personal responsibility, Campbell and I were in unison and he became a frequent guest speaker and supporter of the Progressive Party provincially.

Douglas Campbell and I were more than political colleagues. We were political friends.

❖ PIERRE ELLIOTT TRUDEAU

I had the good fortune to meet and have conversations with Pierre Elliott Trudeau during my years as a cabinet minister. Schreyer had told him about my support, both legally and practically, for the recognition of the French language as one of the official languages of the country.

As soon as I entered the Legislature I began taking French lessons and several of my children took French immersion courses. In 1968 the question of French as an official language of Canada was raised to a new level because of Trudeau's election as Prime Minister. On various occasions I had the opportunity of conversing with him on an official basis at federal-provincial conferences and on a social basis at the various receptions held at those gatherings.

Trudeau was quite gregarious and very open to discussions with those in attendance. His greatest asset was his superior intellect. His greatest fault was his disdain for most other politicians around him. His respect was reserved for the elite few.

An occasion which remains in my mind involved a discussion between Trudeau and several westerners at a reception following a conference. In Winnipeg, during a visit to western Canada, the Prime Minister made the famous statement concerning the Wheat Board. While addressing farmers, he said "Why should I sell your wheat?"

During discussions at the reception, Trudeau insisted that his attitude was quite proper. He saw no reason why the farmers should expect the federal government to make any extra efforts to sell wheat produced by the Western farmer.

I made the observation to Trudeau that if, out of the about 260 seats in the House of Commons, 186 came from the Prairie provinces, the wheat would be sold. Taken aback Trudeau said, "You're not interested in the good of the country, you're a cynic." I responded, "It may be true that I'm a cynic but it is also true that if there were 186 Western seats in the House of Commons, the wheat produced by the Western farmers would be sold." The conversation ended abruptly.

I cannot think of another politician who had a more positive attitude with regard to the danger of ethnic nationalism than Trudeau. He understood such danger to the extent that, in my opinion, it was a major reason why he became politically active in the Liberal party. He observed the danger of Quebec's ethnic French nationalism and entered politics in order to effectively fight it. Many people in the West believed Trudeau wanted to establish French as an official language throughout the country and impose it in areas where it was not wanted. In my opinion, they greatly misunderstood his major motivation.

While Trudeau wanted to protect the interests of French-speaking people in other parts of Canada, he was much more concerned about protecting the interests of English-speaking people in the province of Quebec. It is sometimes forgotten that every initiative he took to protect French in other parts of the country also protected English in the province of Quebec.

Trudeau feared the impact of separation and ethnic French nationalism on the English-speaking people of Quebec, in particular those in West-Montreal where he resided. In my opinion this was his major motivation in fighting separatism but it must be admitted that his fight was largely unsuccessful.

What cannot be disputed is that Rene Levesque and the Parti Quebecois gained more during Prime Minister Trudeau's administration than at any other period.

❖ DAVID LEWIS

David Lewis was, without doubt, the most powerful, influential and able politician in the NDP While Tommy Douglas was the heart and soul of the party, Lewis provided its brain and muscle. Many of Douglas' characteristics found their opposites in Lewis, who was vain, self-centered, gregarious and intensely involved in any intrigue taking place within the party.

Lewis served the party as national secretary, president and vice-president and whatever capacity he wanted, and often succeeded in being the major controller of everything that was going on.

I first met Lewis in the legal, rather than in the political field. A prominent labour lawyer in Toronto, he had acted for most of the major unions in the country. My law office acted for the United Steel Workers which was engaged in an intra-union war with the Union of Mine, Mill and Smelter Workers over who would be the bargaining agent for workers at Thompson's International Nickel Company. The Mine, Mill and Smelter Workers Union jumped the gun and was the first union to be granted certification status by the Manitoba Labour Board.

In the union movement the Mine, Mill and Smelter Workers group was regarded as communist controlled. Lewis prided himself on fighting communists whether in the NDP or the union movement. Therefore it was natural for him to come to Winnipeg and be part of the team acting for the steelworkers when they raided the other union and obtained majority support of the workers in an effort to oust the Smelter Workers group. There is no question about Lewis' ability, capacity and talent as a lawyer just as there is no question about his capacity and talent as a political figure. After several unsuccessful attempts, he was finally elected to the House of Commons in 1965 and was automatically regarded as Douglas' right hand man.

Lewis was an exceedingly able parliamentarian. My differences with him arose after the 1971 election when Robert Stanfield narrowly missed displacing Trudeau as Prime Minister of Canada. As previously indicated, my relationship with Lewis deteriorated after his decisions following that election.

In comparing Douglas and Lewis I would cite the following story. If Douglas was facing a brick wall and wanted to get to the other side he would charge against the wall. He might be successful or he might not be successful, depending on the strength of his charge. Faced with the same situation, Lewis would determine the thickness of the wall, would measure the velocity of his charge and every other conceivable variable and would finally wind up doing nothing. With Douglas there was always a willingness to fight even with the possibility of losing. If there was any possibility of losing, Lewis would find a way to avoid the fight.

❖ BEN HANUSCHAK

Ben Hanuschak and I joined the NDP about the same time. When we ran for municipal office I was elected while he was not.

Because he had been active in the New Democratic organization, when both of us were elected to the legislature in 1966, I as NDP president, recruited him to be the provincial secretary. There is no question that he was one of the most gifted members in the caucus. Hanuschak had a law degree along with a degree in education. He had a farming and a city background. He was fluent in Ukrainian and had been the president of the Red River Co-op and the Winnipeg Teachers Society, both influential and important organizations.

Without a doubt Hanuschak was one of the most clever people I have ever been associated with. His only drawback was a lack of ambition and energy to exploit his talents. In fact he was a laid back individual and took things as they came rather than making things happen. His shrewdness and intelligence, however, were often in evidence and he made considerable contributions to the legislative debate.

In 1968 Hanuschak was the only MLA who refrained from signing the so-called declaration repudiating my attempt to run for the leadership. He supported me in both contests. He also became a founding member of the Progressive Party. He and his wife were a wonderful political team and Nadia's support always contributed to his success.

One example of Hanuschak's peculiar shrewdness occurred in the Legislative Assembly. A Conservative member, Mrs. William Hamilton, who won the seat when her husband died, was making one of her regular temperance speeches. She asked rhetorically, "Do you know that the people of Manitoba paid more for liquor than they paid for education?" Hanuschak interjected, "Lower the price of liquor."

Without a trace of racism, Hanuschak dealt well with the issue of antisemitism which was prevalent with some members of his Ukrainian community. When he supported me for the NDP leadership, an important religious dignitary in that community said to him, "Hanuschak, you're supporting Green." Hanuschak responded, "Yes, I am." The cleric said, "But Green is a Jew." Hanuschak replied, "Don't worry, I'm not supporting him because he's a Jew."

When I was driven out of the NDP, the writing on the wall indicated Hanuschak would be the next to go. He knew it and also knew he could not support the new thrust that appeared to be taking hold of the NDP. He joined the Progressives at considerable cost to himself. It is possible, but unlikely, that he could have continued as a New Democrat. When he become a Progressive he did it at much more risk to himself than I did. I could always return to my law practice. It would have been impossible for Hanuschak to return to the teaching profession. Nevertheless he followed his principles and gave it a supreme effort.

When the Progressives failed, Hanuschak ran for the West Kildonan school board and topped the poll, as he has done in almost every school board election since that time.

❖ PETER TARASKA

As long as I can remember, Peter Taraska was a municipal politician. As a City of Winnipeg alderman when I was a boy, his name was known throughout North Winnipeg and because he was not one of the CCF I always considered him to be the enemy.

I knew him only by reputation until 1962 when I was elected to Metro Council, where he was a member. As a Metro Councillor, he was a dissident who was constantly at odds with the rest of the Council. That image would be reinforced by Saul Cherniack, who sat with Taraska. My opinion of him changed drastically after getting to know him. We became friends and colleagues although we were not on the same side of the political fence.

Taraska, more than any other person whom I met in politics, taught me about the human quality of politics. While he was a sound representative, he also knew the weakness, frailties and vanities of every person with whom he came in contact. Even more importantly, he acknowledged his own frailties.

Taraska's most major coup occurred in regard to the chairmanship of Metro. The Metropolitan Corporation of Greater Winnipeg, which was created by the Roblin administration, consisted of 10 councillors elected in different wards of the City and a chairman, appointed by the provincial government. That person was Dick Bonnycastle, a man of integrity.

As pressure increased to have the chairman elected, Bonnycastle agreed and stepped down. It was then decided that the councillors would elect their own chairman. While Taraska was considered by everyone to be an outsider, by playing upon personal frailties he succeeded in engineering the election of the least likely councillor as the Chairman.

The strong members on Council were Bernie Wolfe, Tom Findlay and Charles Huband. Huband was an outstanding councillor but he had no designs on the chairmanship. In the meantime Taraska realized that while he, Albert Bennett, and Ostrander were outsiders, they had strength in numbers. So he devised a plan whereby Ostrander would become chairman if he pledged not seek to re-election. After receiving that commitment, Taraska obtained enough votes to have Ostrander elected – to the surprise of many fellow-councillors. He not only succeeded in preventing any strong opponent from obtaining the plum position, he succeeded in getting rid of Ostrander who was compelled to keep his pledge not to run again – something he may never have intended to do.

Taraska's astuteness as a politician was apparent in a comment he made at a political conference in the US. When he and elected officials were discussing how judges were appointed, Taraska was intrigued to learn that, in the US, certain judges were elected by the public. He could not understand how a politician could be elected as a judge, since in Canada judges were required by tradition, if not by law, to stay out of any political activity. Indeed until very recently superior court Judges did not have the right to vote.

The discussion continued for some time until Taraska observed, "Now I understand. In the US, in order to be a judge, you have to be an elected politician, while in Canada, in order to be a judge you have to be a defeated politician."

INDEX